Breaking The Code

A Pragmatic Approach to Hope and Change

Jeanine Orzani and Sarah Gleeson

This book is a work of nonfiction. Where individuals are referenced, events are described to the best of the authors' knowledge and recollection. Some identifying details may have been altered for privacy or legal reasons.

First Edition

Published by:

First published in 2026 by The Code Collective

Queensland, Australia

www.reckoningroom.com.au

ISBN: 978-1-7646272-1-4 (Paperback)

ISBN: 978-1-7646272-0-7 (eBook)

Cover design by: Jeanine Orzani

Interior design by: Page Turner Studios Pty Ltd

Library Cataloguing Data

A catalogue record for this book is available from the National Library of Australia.

Printed in Australia.

The views expressed in this book are those of the authors and are based on personal experience, research, and documented records. The publisher assumes no responsibility for errors or omissions. Readers are encouraged to seek professional advice where appropriate.

For David Moyle.

For the courage it takes to speak when silence is safer.

For the cost that comes with telling the truth.

Because what happened should never happened,

and because silence was never an option.

Contents

Acknowledgement

This book exists because harm does not happen by accident.

It happens because someone with authority permits it to continue.

When we first began this work, we never truly believed it would be finished or that it would become real.

Not because we lacked commitment or resolve, but because there were repeated and deliberate blockages placed in our way by others.

In that sense, we acknowledge those who harmed us.

Not in gratitude for what they did, but in recognition of what their actions revealed.

Without them, we would not be the people we are today.

What was taken from us was not small.

Parts of our confidence, our safety, our sense of self, and our trust were stripped away.

But what was taken was not permanent.

We rebuilt.

We relearned.

We re-established ourselves, on our own terms.

What others now say about us no longer carries weight.

Our boundaries are firm, not only in work, but across every part of our lives.

Writing this book was not easy.

There were tears.

There were moments of anger.

There were disagreements between us, and there were times when the material was deeply triggering. At times, it asked us to sit with memories we would have preferred to leave untouched. Yet alongside that difficulty came something else.

Release.

Clarity.

Catharsis.

The act of naming what happened, and placing it into structure and language, was part of reclaiming our own authority.

This book is the result of that process.

It stands as proof that harm can be confronted without being carried forever, and that authorship: of story, of boundaries, of self, is one of the most powerful forms of repair.

We did not write this to seek validation.

We wrote it to tell the truth, and to help others navigate what we were never warned about: systems that harm quietly, authority that goes unchecked, and the long, disorienting aftermath of being permitted to be hurt.

If this book helps even one person recognise what is happening to them sooner, trust their own perception more deeply, or leave a damaging situation with their sense of self intact, then the cost of writing it was worth paying the price.

This is not a story about resilience for its own sake.

It is a record.

A reckoning.

And an offering.

Introduction

The key creators of this book are three former union officials. Their unions remain unnamed to protect those who still strive for good inside the movement. None of us left by choice. We loved ourselves too much to linger in workplaces that thrived on cycles of abuse.

This book gathers stories from our lived experience, as well as insights from other union officials, past and present.

For simplicity, we've rebranded our former employers as:

- Union A
- Union B
- Union C

Names and identifying details have been changed, but the patterns remain unmistakable.

The ways Australian workers are bullied are tragically consistent across industries and demographics: sexual harassment because of gender, exclusion because of age, being silenced because of disability or background.

The labels change, but the abuse follows a familiar script.

It is the same cycle you see in homes where coercive control and family violence take hold: charm, devalue, isolate, punish.

What happens behind closed doors in a household is mirrored in boardrooms, branch offices, and bargaining tables.

This book is not written to sensationalise. It is written to help you recognise the cycle of abuse at work, and to remind you that you are not alone.

About Them

Our former employers, the unions we left behind, preferred a different creed:

Ride on the coattails of others.

About Us

We operate as a team. Our guiding belief is simple:

We stand on the shoulders of giants.

How We Connected

It began with a question.

The employee from Union C asked the employee from Union A, quietly:

"Have you ever felt so alone?"

The employee from Union A answered without hesitation:

"No one should ever feel that way."

Later, the employee from Union C reached out to the employee from Union B through social media and told her that the employee from Union A already knew his story.

At first, the employee from Union B was cautious. She asked the employee from Union A who he was. The employee from Union A explained that this was the person she had spoken about. The one whose experience echoed her own in ways that were impossible to ignore.

That was the moment recognition replaced isolation.

There was no plan, no coordination, no intention to build anything beyond understanding.

What connected us was the unsettling realisation that experiences shared in confidence followed the same structure, the same tactics, and the same outcomes.

We did not find one another through institutions or formal channels. We found one another through honesty.

What followed was alignment, not orchestration. Each of us spoke from our own experience, in our own time, using the platforms available to us.

We underestimated how far those stories would travel once they were no longer told in isolation.

We did not set out to dismantle systems.

We set out to survive, to make sense of what had happened to us, and to ensure that no one else had to navigate it alone.

The rest followed.

The order in which we introduce ourselves is not about seniority, status, or years of service. It is about resilience: who was knocked down first, and how we rose again.

The Employee from Union B

She was the first to fall. With her employment stripped away and her bank balance dwindling, she dedicated two years to rebuilding herself. She read everything she could about workplace bullying and corporate psychopathy. She walked, journalled, practiced yoga, and even created videos on narcissism, trying to make them light enough to laugh through the tears. She refused to build new relationships until she understood the old ones that failed. What looked like solitude was, in fact, preparation. What she was building, unknowingly at the time, was a framework for recognising abuse when it wears professional clothing.

The Employee from Union A

She was next. Forced into an unfair redundancy, her professional reputation dragged through the mud by vexatious claims, not only inside her workplace, but across the wider union and political world. The red-haired renegade, once celebrated for her stamina and drive, was discarded without care for the miles she had driven herself into the ground. In response, she turned two years of her life into research on positive workplace culture, effective policy, and what it truly means to lead up. She didn't just cope, she *analysed*.

The Employee from Union C

He came last, but his fall was no softer. Once a dedicated organiser, he found himself cornered by harassment, ridicule, and a campaign to strip him of dignity. What should have been a safe and collegiate environment became a place of intimidation and unwanted attention. When he sought help, his efforts were met with silence and, at times, hostility. The toll was heavy, not only on his work, but on his sense of safety and belonging.

Like those before him, he refused to let the story end there. His way forward was slower, quieter, but no less determined. He picked up a camera and began to see the world through a new lens.

Photography became his self-care, a way to reclaim focus, frame beauty, and capture moments of stillness in the middle of chaos. What began as survival grew into a practice that grounded him, reminded him of perspective, and allowed him to rebuild piece by piece.

Though our stories began separately, they converge here. We supported each other when institutions turned their backs. On our worst days, when one of us faltered, the others carried the load.

Together, we've come to believe this:

Falling down is inevitable. Getting back up is the only choice.

And now, it's your turn to see what we saw, to know that recovery is possible.

The journey is long, with its peaks and valleys, but one morning you will wake to find yourself smiling again.

We have aimed to present this content as professionally as possible, because that is the standard workers deserve. But experience has taught us that we do not live in Neverland.

At times, coarse language appears in these pages. It has been included deliberately, to preserve the integrity of the stories, and convey the reality of bullying and harassment in the workplace.

Out of respect for the diversity of readers, we have limited this as much as possible. The decision was made collectively, guided by the words of the employee from Union C:

"I'm not here to give you popular advice. I'm here to give you honest advice."

We stand on the shoulders of giants. We don't ride on the coattails of others.

This book is for workers **inside** the system and those already expelled by it.

Prelude

We preface this book with a prelude on the authors and the 'why'. Many, having heard our stories, write us off as disgruntled ex-employees. That's untrue. We were union officials. Our job was to protect workers and slaughter the careers of employers or managers behaving inappropriately. We did. Many of them. But we were also subjected to horrendous mistreatment in the workplace. We write this book, quite simply, for one reason:

If it could happen to us, with a dogmatic approach to workers' rights, what about the lay person?

Where do they stand and what options do they have available?

Nothing. They're stuck.

But hopefully, this book will help change that.

Society labels us as Social Justice Warriors, but when your job is on the line, labels become meaningless. That is the epitome of employment law.

If you are here, reading this, we are so sorry for what has been done to you.

Many people think bullying ends in the formative years. It does not. Those children who throw sand in the play pit go on to do the same in places of employment.

We write this because it is the helping and caring industries that face the worst.

The union movement uses the concept of 'swings and roundabouts'. You are swung around, and use the roundabout rules, only to be faced with a road user who does not obey them.

We live in a society that knows the rules but chooses to actively and without fear of getting caught, disobeys them. This applies in a workplace context and can end in lives lost.

Consider this book your new best friend, as you navigate the uncertainty, backstabbing, and attempts to belittle, and believe what you know to be true.

Our 'why' is simple. We believe in these core values:

- Social justice
- Equality
- To be safe at work
- To be free from harm

And workers have the right to:

- Inclusion
- Safety
- Dignity & Respect
- Collaboration
- Information
- Privacy

A key factor to take into account in reading this book is the premise we live in a *legal* system, not a justice system.

It is given that name as a general catch-all, to capture the parties involved.

These include legal advocates and lawyers; the courts at both a state and federal level; and, in some matters, the police service in each state and territory.

The harsh reality is few achieve true justice within the parameters of the black and white application of law.

It would be a misguided approach to presume trade unions, as torch bearers for workplace justice, are free from inappropriate conduct.

To be clear, unions, as workplaces, are not immune to the effects of bullying and harassing behaviours from individuals within those workplaces.

We, as three former union officials, are turning a negative into a positive by deploying our lived experience, lessons learned, and unique skill sets throughout these pages to support you and help you navigate your way out of a tricky spot.

Three factors sit behind this book.

The first is the idea we are realists.

We are here to offer you hope, however, we are not going to sugar coat the situation or tell you everything is going to be alright. That is gaslighting and, if you've been bullied, then you've already been gaslit into believing you're the problem. You're not.

The second is that we will challenge you.

In trade union terminology it is called *reality testing*. We want you to take action and feel safe to express yourself without fear of reprisal but we will ask you to think through the potential consequences of your actions.

Third, and most important, we will prepare you for the worst.

In the trade union realm it is called: *inoculation*. Many workers, having spent periods of time being treated poorly, can react, with both ferocity and speed, once they have a method to assert themselves. Throwing a rock at the employment boat, however, does not always result in the Titanic-sized sinking the worker had so been anticipating. Often, from experience, the same way the rich and famous were prioritised when the Titanic hit an iceberg, the same happens when abuse of power is exposed at work.

One final consideration to sit with, before you delve into the upcoming content, is the need to be kind to yourself.

If, or when, you realise the role of perpetrator was yours in the past, consider this: *Narcissists are highly manipulative individuals who will go to any length to discredit their target.*

To better understand the narcissist, we have provided some further reading to help buffer your learning journey.

Why Is It Always About You? The Seven Deadly Sins of Narcissism, by Sandy Hotchkiss, is an easy read. It provides relationship contexts for both personal and professional, offering tips on how to handle these types of personalities. Working as a clinical social worker and psychotherapist, Sandy Hotchkiss noted a presentation of repeat symptoms from her clients and established one common factor: Narcissism.

This stands in direct contrast to the work of Thomas Erikson, author of ***Surrounded by Idiots*** and ***Surrounded by Psychopaths***. Erikson demonstrates that poor communication and even malicious behaviour can be understood, not excused, by first understanding one's own personality type. Rather than sensationalising harm, he names it. He explores the darker sides of human behaviour in a way that is clarifying and validating, not re-traumatising. By introducing concepts such as the Dark Triad, his work offers a contained, accessible entry point into understanding destructive personalities without leaving the reader overwhelmed or fearful. *Surrounded by Idiots* is particularly grounding: it reminds you that navigating the world is often difficult, not because you are deficient, but because others are. And that distinction matters.

Furthermore, within the world of narcissistic research, you'll frequently come across a term called: *flying monkey*.

There is a chance you were once used by the narcissist who harmed you, or one of their associates, to gather information on a target.

There is even a chance you had false information given to you or that was "leaked" and then used against the target.

We are not anticipating you becoming an expert in this field.

That would be unrealistic. We are still learning ourselves.

Knowing these terms will make it easier for you to delve into new areas, they may pique your interest, or you'd benefit from learning more.

It is not easy thinking you're the 'bad guy' but when you see things from a victim versus a perpetrator lens, you can quickly flip the reframe and remind yourself you are the victim here, one who was used by the perpetrator to create another victim. But, know this, you are a survivor and not a victim. The goal for this book is to turn you into a thriver, not just a survivor.

We are breaking the code: the unspoken rule that what happens inside unions stays inside unions. If three former union officials, with a combined 27 years of workplace advocacy and a working knowledge of employment law, could be targeted, undermined, and pushed to the edge, and still come to understand that we were never the problem, then this truth matters. Not because our story is unique, but because it is not.

If this book helps even one person recognise what is happening to them, trust their own experience, and reclaim a sense of agency where it was stripped away, then the adversity that led us here was not wasted.

That is why this book exists.

Throughout this book, the authors have assigned a character to each chapter, grouping them by recurring patterns of behaviour.

Some appear innocuous on the surface.

That is their power.

It is often the least likely figures who cause the greatest harm.

These characters include bully managers, enablers, and those who were once victims themselves, alongside the many workers we supported during our time as union officials.

Through these stories, we move beyond the façade and examine what sits beneath it.

If you recognise yourself in these pages, know this: you are not alone.

Others have walked this path before you.

They endured.

And they found a way through.

If we can do it, so can you.

What comes next is the code itself: the rules no one admits to writing, but everyone is expected to follow.

Note: *This book draws on lived experience and professional observation. It does not replace independent legal, medical, or psychological advice. Some sections include brief content warnings, not to soften what follows, but to acknowledge the real psychological and physical harm these experiences can cause, and to allow readers to engage with the material safely.*

Part 1
What Happened

The Code

THE TORMENTOR

The tormentor does not rush. They dismantle their target slowly, publicly, and with intent, turning discomfort into a spectacle and silence into consent.

RIGHT WITH YOU

Introduction

How is it that those with the greatest capacity to inflict harm remain blind to the consequences of their actions?

One harsh truth to own, without pretence or recourse to the utopian ideal that we live in a fair and just world, is this: Bad people do bad things to good people and, more often than not, society blames those harmed for not being strong or resilient enough.

What is worse, and the reason this book is written as it is, is simple: Those with power misuse it to harm the most vulnerable.

They are blind to the consequences of their actions, and to the toll those actions take, not only on their targets, but on those who stand by and try to offer support.

Their conduct, intended, deliberate, and malicious, leaves wounds that take months, sometimes years, to heal. Some never do.

They are who this book was written for.

Before turning to the accounts from Unions A, B, and C, it is important to be clear about how they should be read.

These are not isolated failures, personality conflicts, or unfortunate anomalies.

They are parallel expressions of the same system operating under different conditions.

As you read, notice what repeats: the language used, the silences that follow, the shifting standards, and the inversion of responsibility.

The settings change.

The titles change.

The outcomes do not.

What follows is not about individual organisations, but about a pattern that emerges when power is left unchecked and harm is reframed as weakness.

Union A

This union is legally authorised to protect the rights of predominantly white-collar workers, ranging from those on the lower end of the pay scale to senior managers and executives within large, state-wide organisations.

The former employee's role with Union A was initially administrative in nature and based outside a state capital city. At the time of the events described below, this was not the senior advocacy role from which the employee would later be forced out. During this period, the employee held multiple jobs concurrently. One was with Union A. Others were with separate entities.

The following sequence of events occurred while the employee was working for one of those other entities. It is a true account of:

Power and Control

"Although this story sits outside the union context, it was my union values that alerted me to the harm I was being asked to participate in. I was directed, as the person responsible for administrative tasks, to place a job advertisement to recruit another worker. When I questioned the employer's motive, I was told they wanted to 'shake up' the existing staff. I challenged this, stating it was unethical and immoral. The response was simple: 'You'll do as you're told.'

I felt I had no choice and complied."

The day the advertisement went to print, one of the existing workers took their own life.

Was the advertisement the cause?

Perhaps. Perhaps not.

What is certain is the consequence. The employee carried an enduring sense of responsibility for that death: a burden that remains to this day. It is a permanent reminder that actions have consequences, particularly where vulnerability is present and power is misused.

Just Say No

At first glance, refusing feels like the obvious response. In reality, it is more complex. Under employment law, a worker is required to comply with lawful and reasonable directives. There are limited circumstances in which refusal is permissible. Any request by an employer must be both lawful and reasonable.

In this instance, directing an administrative employee to place a job advertisement was lawful. It was also reasonable. From a legal standpoint, the employee had no grounds to refuse the directive, despite the ethical concerns involved. The emotional impact was real and justified. Legally, however, there was no avenue to contest the instruction.

The Compound Effect

The question is what happens when the same employee later encounters another environment of power and control, not as a single incident, but as a sustained pattern, involving multiple perpetrators.

The section titled The Compound Effect appears in chapters for this reason. In the case of Union A, that effect culminated in mobbing.

Mobbing is a complex and insidious form of workplace abuse. Its cumulative nature makes it difficult to identify while it is occurring. For this reason, and in recognition of workers lost to workplace bullying, an entire chapter of this book is dedicated to unpacking it in detail.

Years Later

Now employed solely by Union A, the same employee was promoted into a direct advocacy role. It was here that power and control again shaped their working life.

Initially, the employee did not recognise the mistreatment. Not because it was subtle, but because it was normalised. The behaviour was not a single incident. It was a sustained environment of bullying, control, undermining, and disrespect.

Only after a prolonged period away from the workplace did the full extent of the mobbing become clear.

Why was it not recognised sooner?

Because the employee had been subjected to gaslighting: a manipulative tactic reinforced through the use of enablers, often referred to as flying monkeys, to distort reality and suppress resistance.

Despite this, the employee instinctively challenged the behaviour at each stage. That resistance did not end with their departure. With clarity restored, they could see the patterns for what they were and chose to continue advocating for change.

This was not performative resistance. It was grounded in core union values. Values that persist, despite the contradiction between the movement's principles of social justice, equality, and care, and the harm tolerated within some of its institutions.

The former employee continues to speak out because silence allows these methods to be repeated. Without challenge, other unsuspecting workers remain at risk.

The Motto:

DO NOTHING. NOTHING CHANGES.

Tip:

Trust your instincts.

Union B

This union is legally authorised to protect workers in highly feminised industries. These workers are deemed "essential" yet are disproportionately characterised by:

- lower rates of pay;
- higher proportions of workers who speak English as a second language;
- higher numbers of workers from countries where gender roles are shaped by rigid, patriarchal norms; and
- limited access to education about workplace rights, making it more difficult to distinguish between genuine gains and hollow promises.

This combination increases vulnerability to emotional blackmail and coercive practices.

Employers within this sector operate across both public and private spheres, ranging from small sites with one or two workers to large corporate entities spread across multiple locations. Lower literacy levels and language barriers complicate recruitment, issue identification, and effective intervention.

In sectors where many workers are unaware that unions exist, membership growth should be exponential. That it does not, speaks volumes.

Some potential members originate from countries where union involvement can result in severe punishment, including execution. While Australian employers may be hostile toward union activity, execution is not an outcome associated with exercising workplace rights here. Even so, fear persists. These workers are frequently employed by the most exploitative operators, where underpayment and missing entitlements trap them in conditions best described as modern labour exploitation.

This same fear-based model was mirrored internally at Union B.

Employees were subjected to excessive workloads, unreasonable demands, and sustained verbal abuse by senior leadership. At times, this abuse escalated into profanity during all-staff meetings, including meetings attended by lower-paid female administrative staff. The behaviour intensified in social settings involving alcohol. Union B's workers, like many of their members, were terrorised into compliance.

Both groups paid the price.

The following sequence of events occurred while employed by Union B, in the role of workplace advocate. It is a true account of:

Excessive Control

Although this account centres on an incident in Canberra, it began earlier, during a presentation by a community sector worker facilitating behaviour-change programs for male perpetrators of domestic and family violence.

She dismantled the familiar excuse without hesitation.

"I just lost control."

Her response was met with laughter.

"You lost control? You smashed household items: hers, not yours. Your golf clubs are untouched. Not a scratch."

"Well, she made me do it."

"So she picked up the cricket bat, put it in your hand, and told you to destroy only her belongings?"

The point was unmistakable. Harm is deliberate.

Whether in the home or the workplace, bullying centres on the intentional imposition of pain. Wanting to hurt someone, physically or emotionally, is not normal. From this point forward, such conduct should be treated as premeditated until proven otherwise.

When safety is at stake, caution is not paranoia.

It is protection.

Just Say No

As a union official, one effective tool was persistence. A phone call, a negotiated outcome, and a follow-up email were often enough to resolve matters.

Workplace bullies, however, are adept at manipulation.

They present as charming and concerned to outsiders while quietly escalating harm behind closed doors.

The affected worker, watching this performance, often fears one more ally being turned against them.

A calm, deliberate refusal, delivered without confrontation, can restore agency. But by the time it becomes necessary, fear has often taken hold. A critical incident, or series of them, conditions the worker into compliance. "No" no longer feels available.

This is how the Yes Cycle forms.

Cumulative harm traps the worker on a psychological treadmill: hypervigilant, exhausted, and waiting for the next blow.

That is why bullied workers do not say no.

Enforcing Fear

A worker with a modified workstation due to repetitive strain injury had been given a small porcelain Lucky Cat by a colleague, complete with a $2 coin: a quiet symbol of support.

After returning from personal leave, the worker found her workstation relocated and the Lucky Cat removed.

Unable to resume work until the station was reassessed, she focused on the violation itself.

Her space had been entered.

Her belongings were removed.

She lodged a bullying and harassment complaint and applied for further leave to manage the emotional impact.

Management reframed the issue:

"She keeps going on about money and her lucky cat. I need to make sure my workers are using their leave appropriately."

Human Resources was drawn into the process. The response was direct:

"There is a bullying complaint involving one of the three people in this room. That person also approves leave. Are you prepared to let this meeting proceed, knowing it may cause further psychological harm?"

The matter was mediated.

The Lucky Cat was returned.

What should have been a simple click-and-approve process became an exercise in control.

The Compound Effect

The Lucky Cat incident triggered a broader power struggle.

Management demanded that the union official and affected worker leave the meeting room.

The intention was clear: discard the worker and reinforce her disposability.

It backfired.

Instead, the worker introduced the union official to five other administrative staff. Only one was a union member. All shared similar experiences of bullying. They sat rigid, scanning the room, watching the door.

When management emerged to find the union official among the staff, panic followed. They were ushered back into the meeting room, only to be sent out again while consultation occurred.

For a brief moment, the power shifted.

Three senior figures stood outside, waiting.

It was not much. But it was enough.

Sometimes, a small disruption is all that is required to fracture fear.

Years Later

This experience, centred on the Lucky Cat and the gross misconduct of senior staff, prepared the Union B employee for what came next.

In the following account, the author describes being confronted with a firearm at work, in a role where its presence was indefensible. He followed The Code to keep his job.

That silence ended his career.

That is the cost of compliance.

The Motto:

I'M IN CHARGE HERE, NOT YOU.

Tip:

Take time out.

Clear thinking is impossible when fear floods the nervous system.

Union C

This union is legally authorised to protect the rights of both blue and white-collar workers, ranging from those on the lower end of the pay scale to senior managers and executives within large, state-wide organisations.

Its membership spans slower-paced public sector entities and extends into the private sector, where values-based branding is often used to emotionally coerce workers into providing unpaid labour.

The former employee's role was that of an industrial advocate.

Although advertised as full-time, the position routinely exceeded standard working hours.

Union work is not confined to an eight-hour day - it is lived.

Unlike the other two employees, however, the official employed by Union C was also elected into their role and was mid-way through a four-year term when they were removed in circumstances that defy belief.

As the saying goes:

You join a trade union to gain workplace rights.

You work for one to lose them.

This union's external reputation for "bully-boy tactics" was matched internally. It did not hesitate to deploy those same methods against one of its own.

Such behaviour has left it increasingly isolated from more progressive unions and has further undermined an already diminished movement operating within a capitalist system and under conservative governments. These contradictions test even the most patient and capable officials when speaking with workers about union membership.

Before proceeding, a trigger warning is required. The following events were dangerous and occurred within the first month of employment at Union C. What follows is a true account.

Note: If you have experienced workplace intimidation, threats to your safety, or coercive control, you are not alone. Support is available. If this section feels activating, consider pausing here and seeking professional or peer support before continuing.

Ultimate Control

Despite extensive experience handling conflict, the author associated with Union B, who writes this account, was unprepared for a disclosure that mirrored their own prior experience involving a firearm in the workplace.

The employee from Union C described the incident.

Given its gravity, quoted material appears in italics to conserve emotional energy, something required when dealing with workplace bullies.

First, some context.

In Australia, probationary employment typically spans three months, sometimes extending to six. During this period, employment can be terminated without reason, though not unlawfully. While probation should function as a mutual assessment, it is overwhelmingly one-sided. Employees strive to succeed, often at personal cost, while early warning signs are dismissed as part of the adjustment process.

By the time the red flags are recognised, investment has already occurred. Leaving feels risky. Staying feels necessary.

It was during this probationary period that the first major incident occurred.

Breaking The Code: complaining about another union official, was unthinkable.

Within union culture, enduring mistreatment was reframed as strength.

Survival equated to legitimacy.

Those who spoke up were relabelled as "the problem."

In this case, the problem arrived with a rifle.

The firearm was not part of any personal protective equipment.

It was placed deliberately on a filing cabinet, ammunition laid beside it. This was not linked to police work, nor was it incidental. The message was intentional.

The offending official paused, turned, and said:

"*It can shoot targets in both the daytime and at night.*

It has a thermal scope."

No threat needed to be spoken.

The presence of the weapon, and the emphasis on its capability, established dominance. A warning shot was unnecessary. The control lay in knowing the potential existed.

This is why this account is titled Ultimate Control.

Just Say No

Refusal, in theory, appears simple. In practice, it was impossible.

The incident occurred during probation.

Complaining would have ended employment.

More critically, it would have breached the most rigid rule in union culture:

Do not break The Code.

The Code is rarely written down.

It does not need to be.

It is enforced through silence, loyalty tests, and the quiet understanding that certain actions, particularly reporting, escalating, or involving external authorities, are seen not as protection, but as betrayal.

When a workplace reaches the point where an employee is too afraid to make basic requests for safety, the environment is already unsafe.

Early exit often leaves no lasting mark on a résumé.

The signs exist to protect you.

Yet, *The Code* teaches something else: endure, absorb, comply.

It is a logic that has resurfaced publicly in recent years, including during formal inquiries, where senior union figures have acknowledged choosing not to involve police or external bodies for fear it would be seen as "*breaching the code*."

The language is familiar.

The reasoning is the same.

Silence is framed as prudence.

Self-protection is reframed as disloyalty.

For the employee of Union C, however, the situation escalated.

And eventually, *The Code* was broken.

Not recklessly.

Not lightly.

But deliberately.

Because when a code exists to protect power rather than people, breaking it is not misconduct.

It is accountability.

We broke *The Code*.

Someone had to.

Years Later

The firearm was only the beginning.

What followed was a sustained campaign of psychological harm, driven by one individual threatened by the presence of a capable, compassionate colleague. Standover tactics replaced professionalism. Intimidation became routine.

Despite prior military service, familiarity with firearms, and personal resilience, the employee from Union C lived with a lifelong hearing impairment resulting from that service.

That disability was weaponised.

He was forced into isolation under the pretext of being "too loud."

Dragged physically from his chair by multiple colleagues, relocated to a separate space, and eventually pushed out of the building altogether, the exclusion was both literal and symbolic.

The isolation had been engineered over time.

In response to repeated complaints about how loudly he spoke, the employee obtained hearing aids. Rather than resolving the situation, this became another point of humiliation.

He was told he was disturbing others, ordered not to sit in the cubicle beside his colleague, and instructed to go downstairs or elsewhere to make phone calls.

From the outset of his employment, he was routinely referred to using slurs about his hearing impairment.

On one occasion, the intimidation escalated further. He was pushed into a conference room, the door locked behind him, and left there alone for more than an hour.

This was not accommodation.

It was a punishment.

Unionists are a minority in Australia.

Union officials even more so.

Being loud is not a flaw. It is an occupational necessity.

Yet here, it was recast as justification for removal.

The Compound Effect

The employee ultimately left the workplace due to legitimate fears for his safety.

Fears that extended beyond the office.

A comprehensive home security system was installed.

It proved necessary.

CCTV footage later captured the union boss, with a lackey in tow, attending the employee's home, and harassing his wife.

What action followed?

None.

With distance from the workplace, the full scale of what had been permitted became clear. The harm was not accidental. It was enabled.

If you are wondering how far a person seeking ultimate control will go, this is the answer.

They do not stop.

The Motto:

BULLYING IS NEVER OK.

Tip:

Never allow a spoken or unspoken code
to convince you that you are less than.
You are worth more.

Adult Bullying

THE RUFFIAN

The Ruffian hides behind humour. They reframe aggression as banter, violence as "just joking," and harm as oversensitivity.

RIGHT WITH YOU

The first step in understanding your experience is simple.

The child who threw sand at you in the second grade does not disappear.

They leave the sandpit, move through the education system, and eventually enter the world of employment, bringing the same behaviour with them.

Only now it wears a title.

One of the first mistakes victims of workplace bullying make is assuming that bullying ends when graduation caps are thrown into the air. That assumption is comforting, but illogical.

Bullying does not dissolve with a certificate.

It matures, adapts, and embeds itself in professional environments where power, hierarchy, and plausible deniability provide cover.

From this point forward, logic is the one tool you will be denied.

You cannot apply it to your workplace bully. They are illogical by design. Confusion is the strategy. Destabilisation is the goal. An uncertain worker, exhausted by contradiction and doubt, cannot speak up.

Before we go any further, we need to establish some ground rules.

Bullying Is Cruel, Not Cool

Bullying is cruel. It is not a personality quirk, a leadership style, or a rite of passage. It is deliberate, harmful behaviour designed to intimidate, destabilise, and diminish another person.

One of the challenges in naming workplace bullying is the deliberate blurring of lines.

Victims are told they are experiencing reasonable management action when, in reality, they are being subjected to patterns of behaviour that would be unacceptable in any other context.

Before we can move forward, it is necessary to be clear about what bullying is, and what it is not.

There is a phrase often repeated without question:

Those who can - do. Those who cannot - teach.

Most of us can name at least one teacher who changed our lives for the better.

That alone should be enough to retire the phrase. If anything, experience suggests a more uncomfortable truth:

Those who can - do. Those who cannot - bully.

This is not an indictment of an entire profession. It is an acknowledgement of where bullying often takes root: in environments that are high-pressure, hierarchical, and poorly governed.

Online forums and support groups are filled with accounts from workers in sectors that are meant to model care, learning, and leadership, yet repeatedly fail to protect their own.

There are stories that would shock the everyday Australian.

Incidents that, if they occurred in front of the people being served - students, patients, clients - would trigger immediate intervention.

Instead, they are dismissed, minimised, or reframed as stress, personality conflict, or a difficult period.

When leadership changes or accountability gaps appear, the behaviour continues unchecked.

With that in mind, the first ground rule is simple:

Be Kind To Yourself

Being bullied is exhausting. Revisiting events, patterns, and memories, particularly when you are already carrying the weight of self-doubt, can be retraumatising.

Pace yourself.

Be patient with yourself.

What you are navigating is not weakness; it is harm.

Words to the Wise

Education is central to breaking free. When bullying is sustained and systemic, one of its most effective weapons is gaslighting: the slow erosion of trust in your own perception. It is what makes rational, capable people begin to wonder whether they are the problem, whether they imagined it, or whether they somehow invited it.

The work of Deb Falzoi, founder of Dignity Together in the United States, has resonated deeply in those moments when even we questioned ourselves, when it felt as though we were the outlier at a gathering we never asked to attend. We weren't. That belief is part of the gaslighting itself.

In creating Dignity Together, Falzoi offers guidance that cuts through the distortion and recentres the target at a critical point in the bullying cycle:

"My advice to other targets: stay strong.

It's not you. It's them.

Keep being the best you you can be.

Keep striving to improve your career in spite of other people's opinions of you."

Credit: *Dignity Together with Deb Falzoi*

That reassurance matters, but it is only the beginning. Knowing it's not you does not immediately undo the damage done by sustained distortion. Gaslighting does not announce itself. It works slowly, reshaping memory, perception, and self-trust until doubt feels rational and confusion feels earned.

To understand how this happens, and why it is so difficult to name while you are inside it, we need to examine gaslighting directly.

Light With Gas?

One of the most complex concepts to grasp in the context of bullying is gaslighting.

The term originates from the 1944 film Gaslight, in which a newlywed opera singer begins to question her sanity. Objects go missing. Lights, powered by gas, dim without explanation. Her husband insists nothing is wrong. In reality, he is deliberately manipulating her environment to make her doubt her own perception.

The objective is simple: destabilisation through self-distrust.

Disturbing, yes, but clear.

Workplace bullying is rarely that overt.

In some cases, it is.

There are bullies who are brazen, cruel, and unmistakable: those who tell their targets, publicly and without consequence, to go home and kill themselves. That behaviour is horrifying, but it is also easier to identify.

The more insidious version is harder to name and far more damaging.

Before you disengage because you can't relate to such extremes, pause. Subtle gaslighting does more harm precisely because it is difficult to pinpoint. The human brain recognises cruelty when it sees it. What it struggles to comprehend is why another person would behave that way; especially a colleague, a manager, or someone cloaked in authority.

That gap between what you sense and what you can explain is where gaslighting takes hold. Doubt replaces certainty. Confusion begins to feel rational. You start questioning not their behaviour, but your own interpretation of it.

This is a distinct and critical part of the bullying experience. We will return to it later. For now, let's ground this in something concrete.

Let's look at an example.

The Aged Care Worker

Meet AGW. Short for Aged Care Worker.

If you are familiar with the aged care sector, you will know that many workers come from countries outside Australia, speak English as a second language, and enter workplaces with little understanding of their rights. This imbalance is not incidental. It is frequently exploited.

The worker at the centre of this example is a woman in her mid-twenties. She is skilled, qualified, and deeply committed to the care of those she is paid to protect. Her experience unfolds at the end of a long and exhausting legal process, triggered after she raised concerns about bullying and harassment by a manager. That behaviour was concealed by two supervisors, later absorbed into the "in-group," and eventually redeployed against her.

By the time the union official involved with AGW, pulled from an online forum discussing workplace bullying, she was in visible distress. She disclosed thoughts of ending her life. Intervention at that point was not procedural; it was human. Coping strategies were put in place. Support was stabilising. Months later, when the legal matter finally concluded and documentation was signed, AGW returned to the same forum. This time relieved, optimistic, and hopeful that the worst was behind her.

It wasn't.

Two months later, she was back, frustrated, angry, still professional, but now carrying the familiar weight of being the only one forced to put concerns in writing. A nurse, known for repeated bullying behaviour, had verbally abused the core group again. Three colleagues raised concerns verbally. AGW, guided by history, lodged hers in writing.

Human Resources responded that one written complaint was insufficient to constitute bullying.

The others, despite reporting the behaviour to supervisors, were discounted. A minor and irrelevant technicality was used to justify inaction.

An excerpt from the email is below:

"I understand that you felt well supported by the NIC on the day, which is pleasing to hear. Meanwhile we will remind staff at team meetings/training sessions that colleagues need to remember to treat each other with respect and civility, that we aim to offer our clients."

The Nurse in Charge (NIC), was one of several staff who had raised concerns. But because those concerns were not documented "correctly," the employer treated them as if they did not exist. At best, this reflects administrative laziness. At worst, and more accurately, it reflects a calculated decision: it is easier to leave the complainant exposed than to acknowledge a systemic problem.

Each time an employer fails to act, their exposure to negligence increases. That this continues to occur, despite full awareness of the risk, speaks volumes about how workplace bullying is managed in modern Australia.

We asked you earlier to leave logic behind. Now you can see why.

The person who raised inappropriate conduct is quietly repositioned as the problem, formally reminded to behave appropriately, while the behaviour itself goes untouched. Human Resources know how this plays out. Once a worker becomes "the one who complains," they are no longer seen as credible. They are seen as inconvenient.

The bully, meanwhile, understands the rules perfectly. They know they are untouchable. Escalation follows.

The victim knows what is coming next. There are no celebrations here, only anticipation. The only uncertainty is the degree of damage inflicted before the worker leaves.

One ethical question remains. If you are trained to save employment, protect workers, and prevent harm, can you end the career of a bully without hesitation?

This dilemma is often described as The Trolley Problem.

Do you divert the trolley and sacrifice one to save many, or do you allow it to continue unchecked, knowing others will be harmed? For advocates, the decision is rarely abstract. The bully rarely agrees. And that resistance is one reason unions and union officials attract hostility.

For those who value justice and protection of the vulnerable, the work is understood. Sometimes, even revered.

Fight, Flight, Freeze and the Window of Tolerance

When the body perceives threat, it does not stop to analyse intent, context, or fairness. It reacts.

This reaction is governed by the autonomic nervous system and is commonly described as fight, flight, or freeze.

These are not choices. They are automatic survival responses, designed to keep a human being alive in the presence of danger.

In healthy environments, the body activates these responses briefly, then returns to a regulated state. In bullying environments, however, the threat does not pass.

It repeats.

And so the body stays activated.

This is where the concept of the Window of Tolerance becomes critical.

The Window of Tolerance refers to the zone in which a person can think clearly, regulate emotion, and respond proportionately to stress. When inside this window, individuals are able to problem-solve, communicate, and perform their roles effectively.

Workplace bullying systematically pushes people outside this window.

Hyperarousal: Fight or Flight

When stress levels rise beyond tolerance, the body enters a state of hyperarousal. This is commonly experienced as:

- Heightened anxiety
- Irritability or anger
- Hypervigilance
- Racing thoughts
- Difficulty sleeping
- A sense of being constantly "on edge"

In this state, a person may appear reactive, defensive, or emotional. Importantly, this is often the phase that bullies actively provoke. Why?

Because visible reactions can later be reframed as instability, aggression, or poor performance.

Hypoarousal: Freeze

When the stress becomes overwhelming or inescapable, the nervous system may swing the other way into hypoarousal, often referred to as freeze.

This can look like:

- Emotional numbness
- Withdrawal
- Fatigue
- Brain fog
- Low motivation
- Disconnection from others

At this stage, the individual may be labelled disengaged, lazy, or uncommitted. In reality, the body has shifted into conservation mode. It is no longer trying to fight or flee. It is trying to endure.

Why This Matters in Workplace Bullying

What distinguishes workplace bullying from everyday stress is not intensity alone. It is duration and intent.

When stress is engineered and sustained, the nervous system is repeatedly forced outside its window of tolerance.

Over time, this erodes a person's capacity to self-regulate, think clearly, and advocate for themselves.

Reactions that are later criticised were not the cause of the problem; they were the outcome.

Understanding this framework reframes the narrative.

You were not "too sensitive."

You were responding to a threat.

Your body did exactly what it was designed to do.

A Foundation for What Comes Next

As we move forward, this lens becomes essential.

The behaviours discussed in the next chapter: fatigue, overwork, compliance, and dangerous levels of exhaustion, do not arise because people lack resilience. They arise because the nervous system, pushed beyond tolerance for too long, adapts in the only ways it knows how.

This is not a failure of character.

It is a predictable human response to sustained pressure.

Before we name specific symptoms, we need to pause here.

When the body has been operating outside its window of tolerance for a long time, the first and most necessary response is not action.

It is recognition.

And where intervention matters.

The Intervention

If you are reading this and recognising yourself, pause.

This is not the point of action. This is the point of gentleness.

You have likely been holding your body rigid for longer than you realise.

The world may feel jarring, unsafe, or overwhelming.

Let yourself slow down. Let the tears come, if they need to.

What is falling away now is not weakness, it is residue from harm you should never have had to carry.

The next part of this chapter shifts focus.

We move from behaviour to impact.

From patterns to symptoms.

The responses you are experiencing are not personal failings.

They are predictable physiological and psychological reactions to sustained bullying and harassment.

They are unpleasant, but they are understandable.

And they are manageable.

There is no judgement here. You have endured enough of that already.

To understand what comes next, we must first name what the body and mind have been doing to survive.

That is where we begin.

Anxiety

The most common response to workplace bullying is anxiety.

At one end of the spectrum, anxiety may meet the threshold for clinical diagnosis.

At the other, it appears as a series of internal signals, often unnamed, but unmistakable.

Common descriptions include:

- Nervousness
- A sense of threat or danger
- Persistent worry
- Distress
- Agitation
- An automatic protective response

You may experience tightness in your chest, a sense of foreboding without a clear cause, or an inner knowing that something is coming.

The threat may be real or anticipated, but if you are being bullied, it is rarely imagined.

You see the bully approach.

You hear the phone ring.

A message arrives.

Your body reacts before your mind has time to reason.

This is not a weakness. It is your nervous system doing its job.

You cannot control another person's behaviour.

What you can influence, once you understand what is happening inside your body, is how you respond rather than react.

That distinction matters.

And it becomes possible only when you recognise anxiety for what it is: a physiological response to sustained threat.

What Is Happening in the Body

Anxiety is commonly associated with activation of the sympathetic nervous system, often simplified as fight or flight.

Human responses are more nuanced than this, and we will return to that later, but this framework is useful as a starting point.

Anxiety often follows a predictable pattern.

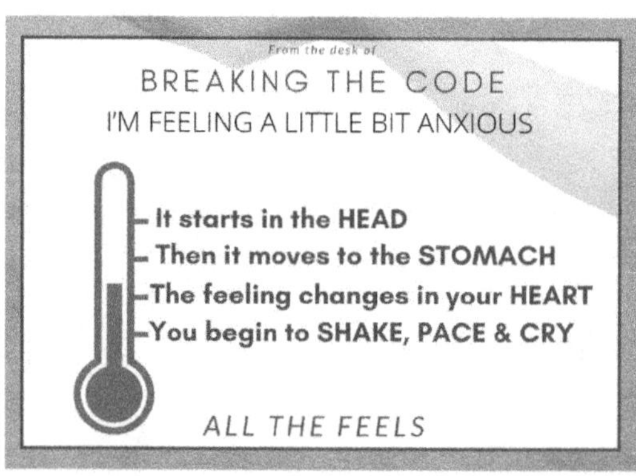

It begins in the mind.

Then moves to the stomach.

The sensations shifts into the chest.

The body mobilises: shaking, pacing, tears. Seeing this sequence matters.

It gives language to something that often feels overwhelming and uncontrollable.

Why Awareness Matters at Work

Workplace bullies rely on reaction.

Not because emotion is wrong, but because emotion can be weaponised. Displays of distress are later reframed as instability.

This is how the "crazy card" gets played.

Once that narrative takes hold, it becomes easier to question your credibility, your competence, or your fitness for work.

This does not mean you are responsible for managing someone else's cruelty.

It means understanding the environment you are operating in, and why emotional safety becomes a strategic concern in unsafe workplaces.

Awareness is not suppression.

It is protection.

Managing Anxiety

Anxiety can be managed, not eliminated, with the right tools.

Common strategies include:

- Regulated breathing for set counts
- Reducing caffeine intake
- Gentle movement such as walking or yoga
- Exploring evidence-based emotional release methods

These are not cures, but supports.

Tools that help settle the nervous system so you can regain choice in how you respond.

There is no judgement here. You have already been judged enough.

Understanding anxiety is not about fixing yourself.

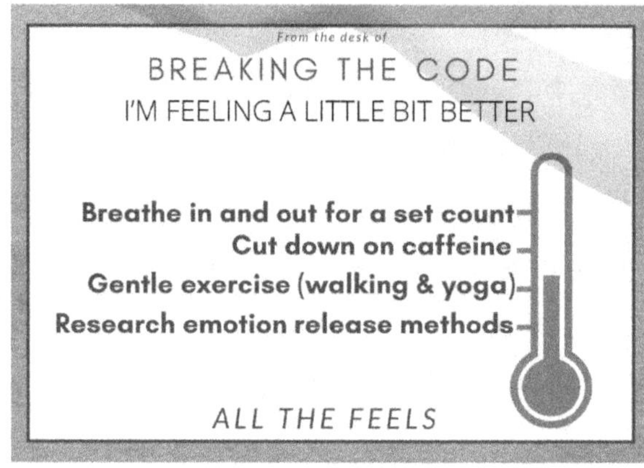

It is about recognising the cost, of what you have been carrying, and learning how to put some of it down.

Transition Forward

Anxiety is only one response.

As exposure continues, the body and mind adapt in other ways.

Some quieter, some heavier.

To understand the full impact of workplace bullying, we now turn to the next common response.

Stress

The second common response to workplace bullying is stress.

In everyday life, stress is usually episodic. It arises from time pressures, financial considerations, or interpersonal conflict.

It comes and goes. It resolves. It does not usually threaten a person's sense of safety or identity.

For clarity, stress is often described in three broad categories:

- Stress imposed by others (family, friends, industry, society, government)
- Stress imposed by yourself
- Stress imposed by your role

What distinguishes workplace bullying is that stress is no longer incidental. It is engineered. When a workplace bully is involved, often a manager, the stress experienced by the target is not a by-product of work. It is the mechanism. Common sources include:

- Excessive workloads
- Unfair expectations
- Unreasonable or shifting demands
- Cruel or belittling comments
- Information overload and nitpicking
- Persistent, unnecessary criticism
- Clinical or dismissive responses to emotion
- Introducing unrelated issues to confuse or discredit
- Pressure to perform tasks outside your role
- Unwanted touching
- Targeted “jokes”
- Threats, humiliation, or verbal abuse
- Moving goalposts
- Micromanagement
- Unreasonable denial of leave

This list is not exhaustive. What it reliably produces is a predictable internal state:

- Degradation
- Humiliation
- Intimidation
- Offence
- Threat
- Exhaustion
- Debilitation
- Undermining
- Victimisation

This is not accidental.

Why Stress Is the Chosen Weapon

We could list stress-management techniques here.

That would miss the point.

The question is not how to cope with stress, but why stress is being deliberately created.

Victims often describe feeling as though they are "walking on eggshells."

Hyper-vigilance sets in. Attention narrows. Decision-making becomes reactive.

This is not personality.

It is the effect of coercive control.

This cycle does not rely on one event.

It relies on accumulation.

Stress escalates until a reaction is inevitable.

Once the target reacts, the narrative flips.

The bully positions themselves as the victim, and the original harm disappears from view.

This is why the stress associated with bullying must not be confused with general job pressure or performance anxiety.

It is systematic pressure, applied for a specific outcome: to provoke an overreaction that can later be used as evidence against you.

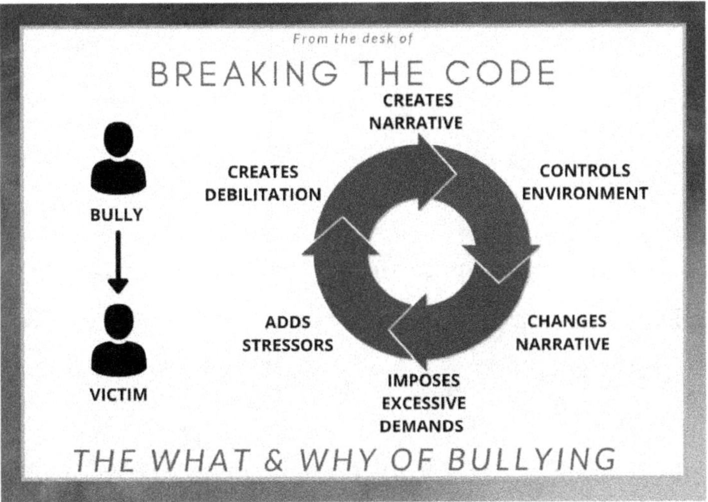

"I'm Not Touching You"

To understand motive, it helps to revisit a familiar childhood pattern.

One sibling moves a finger close to another, close enough to intrude, not close enough to be "at fault."

The targeted sibling eventually reacts.

The instigator, now injured, calls for authority.

The wrong child is reprimanded.

The same dynamic plays out in adult workplaces.

The person who reacts is labelled:

- Angry
- Crazy
- Deluded
- Inappropriate
- Over-emotional
- Reactive
- Sensitive
- Unstable

Attention shifts away from the instigator. The real behaviour goes unscrutinised. The distraction works.

That is the benefit.

A deflection.

The bully is reframed as tolerant. The target becomes the problem. One is elevated; the other is scapegoated.

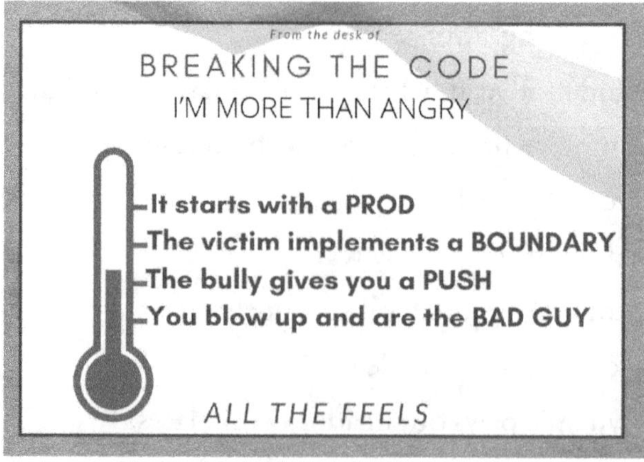

When You Can't Walk Away

There are times when leaving is not immediately possible.

No Contact is the end goal, but not always the starting point.

What follows are protective positioning strategies, not behavioural corrections.

They are about limiting exposure while you regain stability and options.

Upbeat Okay

When a request is designed to provoke, excessive politeness and enthusiasm can interrupt the pattern.

Agreement without emotional investment leaves nothing to grip.

No resistance.

No visible distress.

No narrative to twist.

You are not appeasing.

You are removing fuel.

Superficial Only

Workplace bullies collect information. Emotional, personal, relational.

Keep responses neutral, vague, and surface-level.

This is not dishonesty.

It is containment.

Conversation stays professional. Nothing usable is offered.

A Little Leak

Where triangulation is suspected, low-value information can be used diagnostically.

If it returns to you, the channel is identified.

Awareness increases.

Exposure decreases.

These strategies are not about winning.

They are about reducing harm while you plan your exit or escalation.

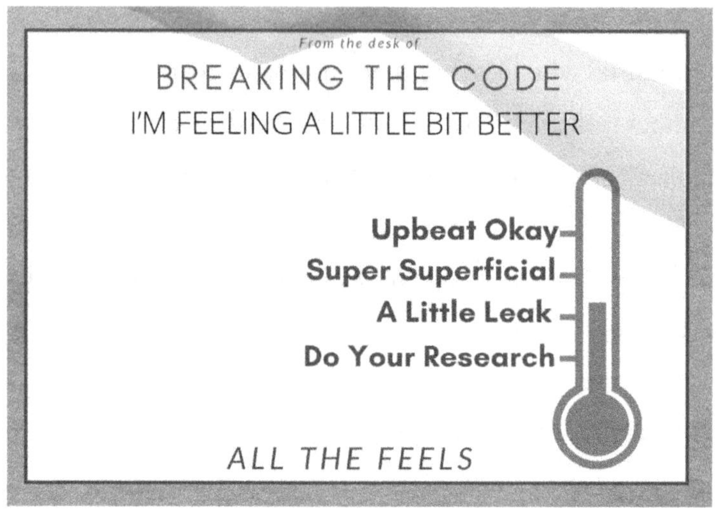

Before We Move On

Stress in bullying is not about resilience.

It is not about better time management.

It is not about thicker skin.

It is about sustained pressure applied until the body, mind, or reputation gives way.

Understanding this matters, because stress is often the bridge between anxiety and what comes next.

That is where we turn now.

Depression

When anxiety and stress remain unchecked, a third response may emerge: depression.

Depression is not a bad day.

It is not simply sadness or loneliness.

It is a serious mental health condition that affects how a person thinks, feels, functions, and relates to the world around them.

Its impact is often felt across four interconnected domains:

1. Thoughts

Confusion, difficulty concentrating, impaired memory, harsh self-criticism, indecision, and, in some cases, thoughts of self-harm or suicide.

2. Emotions

Anger, shame, sadness, hopelessness, irritability, impatience, emotional numbness.

3. Physiology

Body pain, disrupted sleep, changes in appetite or weight, fatigue, loss of energy, reduced motivation.

4. Behaviour

Withdrawal, agitation or slowing down, crying, shaking, avoidance of people or responsibilities.

These are not personal failings.

They are predictable outcomes of sustained psychological harm.

Those who bully understand this.

Confusion, exhaustion, and emotional depletion impair functional capacity. Over time, the result is brain fog: a sense of moving through life as though caught in something sticky, obscuring, and hard to escape.

Not because you are weak.

But because the environment has been made unsafe.

When the World Shrinks

As depression deepens, self-doubt grows.

You may begin avoiding places, people, or situations that once felt manageable.

Guilt and shame creep in.

Motivation fades.

Sleep becomes fragmented, either elusive or excessive.

Appetite shifts.

Concentration falters.

What once felt like enthusiasm now feels unreachable.

This is the hill many describe as insurmountable: hopelessness.

This is not where we leave you.

But it is where we pause, acknowledge, and orient.

The Need for Balance

Breaking the cycle of depression requires more than endurance.

It requires re-establishing balance: gradually, deliberately, and with compassion.

In union environments, this is often summarised as:

WORK — LIFE — BALANCE

But balance is not a slogan. It is a structure.

Traditionally, the working day has been framed as:

- 8 hours work
- 8 hours life
- 8 hours rest

This structure did not arise by accident.

Early employment law, rooted in the Masters and Servants framework, created extreme power imbalances between employer and worker.

It was only through collective action and union advocacy that workers secured humane limits, including the eight-hour day.

Today's standard 38-hour week appears reasonable on paper.

In practice, when commuting time, unpaid overtime, and emotional labour are factored in, the "life" component is often the first to disappear.

And once life erodes, depression deepens.

What "Life" Actually Contains

The eight hours outside work and sleep are not discretionary. They are essential.

They include:

- Basic care: showering, eating, cleaning
- Movement and exercise
- Hobbies and creative outlets
- Mindfulness or spiritual practices
- Social connection
- Family, partners, children, pets
- Learning and development
- Rest, celebration, and joy
- Volunteering or purpose-driven activity

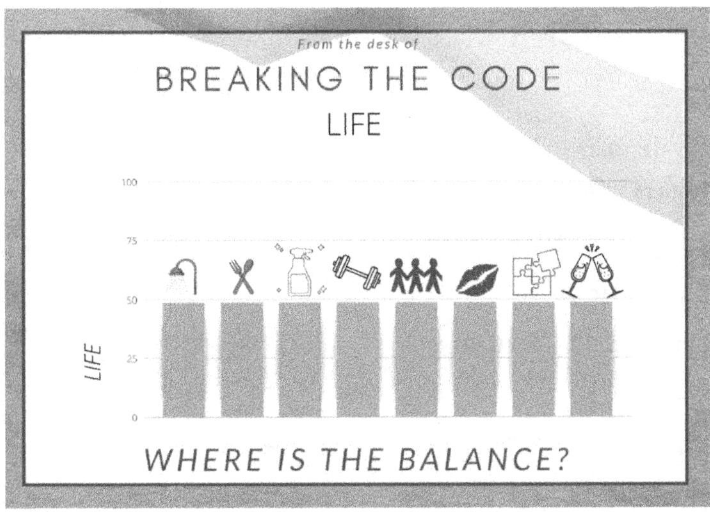

When bullying intrudes, these are the first casualties.

Perspective matters.

Commute time alone can consume a large portion of "life."

Shift work compounds harm.

And the modern reframing of workers from people to resources, under banners like "People & Culture", has not changed the underlying reality: Human Resources exists to manage risk for employers, not to protect employees.

That mistrust is earned.

Moving Forward

If you find yourself here, pause.

You do not need to solve everything today.

You do not need to fix yourself.

You need space to breathe.

If possible, take leave. Step back. Assess where you are.

Imagine yourself as a cup of water; already full, already carrying more than your share.

Each demand, each criticism, each circular conversation causes more to spill. Eventually, there is nothing left to give.

Stop.

Wait.

Collect yourself.

Refilling the cup takes time. Patience. Balance.

Our guiding principle is simple:

One day at a time.

Sometimes one hour at a time.

Not yesterday.

Not tomorrow.

Just now.

Tip:

Reflect on your boundaries.

Clarify your values.

Listen to your intuition.

Practise assertiveness where it is safe to do so.

You are not broken. You are responding to harm.

And that is where healing begins.

Anxiety, stress, and depression do not arise in isolation.

They are responses to sustained pressure applied over time, often normalised, minimised, or reframed as "just part of the job."

By the time the body begins to signal that something is wrong, the environment that caused the harm has already been operating unchecked for far too long.

What comes next, is not always, collapse.

More often, it is compliance; showing up tired, swallowing discomfort, pushing through exhaustion, and doing what is asked because saying no, no longer feels safe.

In the next chapter, The Red Eye, we move from the internal cost of bullying to the visible behaviours it produces, examining how fatigue, overwork, and constant motion become both a survival strategy and a warning sign; one that too many workplaces choose to ignore.

The Red Eye

THE HARASSER

The Harasser calls surveillance care. They watch, track, and nitpick until you learn to live on alert.

RIGHT WITH YOU

This is a story about the most insidious method an employer uses to maintain power and control.

It is done without you even realising it.

That is what makes these types of people so enraged if, or when, they are exposed.

Excessive workload is the facade, one that disguises the toxic employer's insatiable desire to micromanage.

No one likes a micromanager.

They are the party poopers, the fun police and we all have that one thing in common:

Life is about having fun.

They are aware though. With the knowledge only anal retentive people need a microscope to manage, this type overloads you with so much work you don't realise they're inherently boring and incompetent. We know, it's not a good combination. For this chapter we're going to break it down by state and introduce some union-only terminology for you. That said, it is likely to apply to other industries. With a broader brushstroke approach you'll be able to apply it to other areas of your life. It is the idea that you have one area, one area only and you don't move beyond it. As officials, that area was more than enough.

You'll see why, as you read on. The concepts in this chapter will capture the roles imposed upon you, based on upbringing, societal expectations or even factors such as gender and where you sit in the family structure. One author of this book, was told they were a "people person." It was up to them to smile nice and make small talk. As we noted, there are times where roles, with associated parameters, are pressured upon. On that note, let's break down two key phrases you'll find come up frequently in Chapter 3:

Patch

The Area of Responsibility (AOR)

In union roles, an Area of Responsibility refers to the geographic footprint assigned to an organiser. In regional and remote contexts, this can span thousands of kilometres and include isolated communities with limited transport options, unreliable connectivity, and heightened cultural and political complexity. Travel within an AOR is not incidental; it is intrinsic to the role.

These terms common in the unions, are the misguided belief you are in charge of your work life. Nothing is furthest from the truth. Union members, paying their set fees each week, argued they were the boss of you. That's incorrect. The boss is the boss of you. They're the ones doing backroom deals and deciding which side they lie on.

The member-focused funds would connect with their members in a genuine way. Those associated with the political parties, both left and right, would let the power players dictate the agenda and go from there. The officials writing this book are known as:

Rank & File

We are the workers who came from the field and have real world experience in the workforce, like actual workers who have worked in other jobs and industries. This is in comparison to union officials who studied politics or law at university and moved into a career in the union movement. Don't assume bitterness on our behalf. A person with a desire for justice, teamed with the ability to think and research, is a scary adversary. We appreciate the fear when they were on our side. Most were anything but. Those who excelled at law did not work for a trade union, they went into private practice. The others, not so legally inclined, studied politics. They liked the ideal of justice. Too lazy to follow through, they refused to enforce the law. In a system stacked in the employer's favour, it was a recipe for disaster with its enforcement. This character, the highly educated but inept or very sheltered but on the money, will feature heavily in the following text of The Red Eye.

Union A

Packed & Ready To Go

This is the story of Packed & Ready To Go. The key component is the GO. It is about how employers fail to understand the realities of working in regional and remote Australia. They establish a pre-determined status associated with geography and then diminish people on the basis of it.

Regional.

Remote.

Peripheral.

Useful, but never central.

The employee from Union A's bag was always half-packed by the door.

Travel was not a disruption; it was the job. They moved constantly across their Area of Responsibility, which extended from Townsville north to the Cape and west to Mount Isa, excluding Charters Towers and Hughenden. It was a vast geographical footprint, encompassing remote communities, regional centres, and isolated worksites. Places where representation could not be done from a distance.

Presence mattered.

Being in the room mattered.

They arrived early, stayed late, and made themselves available because that was what the role required. Travel was embedded into ordinary working days, not treated as exceptional or separate from the work itself. Movement across Queensland was routine, expected, and, for a time, valued.

And the employee from Union A was not the only one doing it.

There were other organisers based in regional Queensland, another in Townsville, and one in Rockhampton, who carried similar travel loads. Movement across vast distances was not exceptional. It was built into how the work was structured for those outside the metropolitan head-office city. Regional organisers were expected to absorb the kilometres, the fatigue, and the disruption as part of the role.

At the time, this wasn't questioned.

It was understood.

For a while, that presence was valued.

They were invited.

Included.

Trusted.

The kind of worker who could be relied upon to just get on with it.

Then the status shifted.

Not overnight.

Not explicitly.

Quietly.

The social invitations stopped first.

The informal catch-ups.

The conversations that happened before and after meetings. The ones where decisions were softened, aligned, or quietly shaped.

They were still expected to travel, but no longer expected to belong.

The same movement that once signalled commitment was reinterpreted as inconvenience. The same presence that had been required was suddenly framed as optional, excessive, or suspect. City-centric logic began to dominate: *just fly in, just fly out, just make it work*. There was no consideration of distance, fatigue, weather, or the realities of regional travel.

Attendance at Head Office became "necessary," but staying overnight was framed as unreasonable. Flying in early and returning late the same day became the expectation, regardless of the toll. When the employee from Union A challenged this, the response was not practical, it was personal. Why did they need to be there? Why couldn't they manage like everyone else?

Not everyone was regional.

And when the travel burden borne by regional organisers was later scrutinised, that scrutiny was not applied evenly. What had once been a shared, structural expectation was selectively reframed. Approved movement was retrospectively moralised. Necessary presence became something to justify.

The cycle followed a familiar pattern.

Pressure was applied.

The employee from Union A reacted, on behalf of the regional organisers, because the demand was unreasonable.

The reaction was reframed as an overreaction.

Then came the expectation to smooth things over, to apologise, to make amends for responding at all.

React.

Overreact.

Repair.

Over time, the lesson becomes clear.

Don't push back.

Don't question.

Don't show fatigue.

Smile.

Be agreeable.

Be grateful.

The work does not change.

Only the story told about you does.

To survive it, the employee from Union A had to find ways not to harden. Not to let resentment calcify into hatred, of the organisation, the work, or people more broadly. They focused on movement that wasn't imposed. Walking. Small routines. Moments of humour, where they could find them. Reminding themselves that this wasn't the whole world, just a distorted corner of it.

Union A's employee had kept their bags packed. But they began to understand what it cost.

What the workplan makes visible, in hindsight, is the number of hours embedded in that travel. Days routinely began before sunrise and ended late in the evening, particularly during enterprise bargaining periods.

Travel was treated as incidental to the role, rather than labour in its own right.

Despite this, remuneration remained fixed at 35 hours per week. There was no overtime, no time in lieu, and no structural recognition of extended days. The expectation was that regional organisers would absorb the additional hours quietly, until the same travel, particularly the travel allowances, were later reframed as excessive.

Just Say No

It is not easy to say no when a person has been conditioned to feel less than. By the time the ABCDE cycle has taken hold, confidence is already compromised. Instincts are doubted. Reasonable boundaries are second-guessed.

The internal narrative shifts: difficult, sensitive, ungrateful. Saying no feels risky, even disloyal.

One way to interrupt that pattern is through deliberate re-engagement with life outside the role. Not in grand gestures, but through movement. Activity. Laughter. Returning to things that once felt expansive rather than diminishing. The goal is not resistance. It is rebalancing.

Choose one activity - new or familiar. Commit to it a set number of times each week. Move the body. Change the environment. Let joy, even briefly, disrupt the narrative that worth is measured by compliance.

The Compound Effect

What makes this form of travel abuse insidious is not any single trip or demand, but the accumulation. Each concession seems minor. Each adjustment is temporary. Each compromise is survivable. Until it isn't.

The body absorbs what the organisation denies. Fatigue becomes normal. Disconnection creeps in quietly. The cost becomes invisible because giving has become routine.

That is the compound effect.

Years Later

It took time for the pattern to become clear. The travel itself was never the issue. It was necessary, strategic, and shared. What changed was how it was later used: selectively reframed as excess, as indulgence, as evidence of character rather than structure.

That reframing had nothing to do with kilometres travelled or allowances claimed. It had everything to do with power, proximity, and who was permitted to move without consequence.

The Motto:

When a system depends on your movement, it will praise it, until it needs a reason to diminish you.

Tip:

If a practice is normalised across a group but later used against one person, the issue is not the practice. It is the narrative shift.

Document patterns, not just incidents. Time has a way of revealing what was never personal to begin with.

Union B

Pack Your Bags & Go

The following sequence of events, while employed by Union B in the role of workplace advocate, is a true account.

Every Sunday followed the same rhythm:

A self-defence class on Sydney's north side, a return home to pack, then a four-hour drive south.

That description, however, is too neat. To understand how this became routine, it is necessary to rewind.

Once regarded as a high performer, the employee from Union B left the organisation physically incapacitated and unable to work following prolonged and systematic bullying by three women, aided and abetted by a senior male who sexually harassed and touched her. That criminal conduct, the subject of a later book in the making, remains outside the scope of this chapter. What matters here is that the transfer to the ACT marked the moment the bond between employee and employer fractured beyond repair. At the time, the employee did not recognise excessive travel as an abuse mechanism. The first casualty was joy. A volunteer role at an animal shelter, Saturday mornings spent with like-minded people, became impossible. One small, life-giving activity quietly disappeared. Based out of the ACT, the daily grind of Sydney traffic receded. It felt, briefly, like relief. That illusion was short-lived.

The Backfill

"It's only for six weeks. You'll earn full-time wages. The Organiser is on Workers Compensation. We're getting complaints. I don't care if you drive or fly, we need you there Monday."

The red flags were unmistakable in hindsight:

1. The absent Organiser was off on Workers Compensation for psychological injury. He later accepted a cash settlement and withdrew his claim.

2. He had been absent since November 2018. The directive above was issued on 18 January 2019.

3. The Area of Responsibility had effectively been abandoned. Over nine months, the employee from Union B was repeatedly "dragged on," pulled from breaks, pursued into cafés, and loaded with urgent legal matters.

4. The weekly four-hour commute erased any remaining capacity for social life, exercise, or intimacy. One self-defence class remained. Everything else fell away.

The Red Eye Directive

On one occasion, while working in the ACT, the Organiser was directed to attend a site four hours south for a meeting with workers who had already been made redundant.

At the same time, a meeting with the ACT Government, one with outcomes affecting thousands of workers, was scheduled.

The Organiser raised the risk plainly.

"I'll only get four hours of sleep. It's a four-hour drive. It's dangerous."

The direction stood.

The Organiser left Canberra at 4:00 a.m. to comply with the instruction.

On the drive, she experienced a microsleep.

She could have crashed.

She could have died.

What made the directive worse was its futility. The workers at the site had already lost their jobs. Funding had been withdrawn. The service had closed. No alternative outcome was possible. A Legal Officer had already dialled in from the Head Office and was managing the matter.

The justification offered later was that the Organiser's manager needed to stop bullying.

That was not the reality.

The reality was simpler and more revealing: the meeting deemed "essential" was to be attended by three tall, muscular men. Presence, not outcomes, was the objective.

Risk was imposed deliberately. Fatigue was collateral. Control was the point.

Just Say No

The employee eventually did say no; too late, and under surveillance.

While employers may lawfully monitor communications where grounds exist, monitoring driven by romantic obsession does not meet that threshold. The male member of management fixated on the employee accessed call records and emails, and her work-issued device tracked her movements continuously.

The refusal was unambiguous:

"I'm not comfortable with this. You have a partner and two children. Your focus needs to be on them."

The response was not acceptance, but displacement. A stint interstate became preferable to the perceived threat of the employee forming a relationship elsewhere. The employee rejected the offer of becoming a stepmother. The rejection did not matter. The narrative had already been rewritten.

The Organiser on Workers Compensation never returned.

Just Submit Your Fucking Application

Nine months later, after repeated attempts to negotiate a return to Sydney, the pressure escalated. The employee sought to remain in the ACT, where a full-time role was available. Two Sydney roles were advertised simultaneously. None provided a safe alternative.

The directive was issued, not requested:

"Just submit your fucking application."

Compliance followed: delayed, deliberate, and limited. Submission was demanded. Obedience was not guaranteed.

Maintaining Power

Once Sydney-based again, control mechanisms tightened. Weekly meetings required in-person attendance at Headquarters. Other team members were relegated to dial-in participation. Proximity was managed.

Exposure to a bullying manager and an incompetent Industrial Officer created a chronic state of hyper-vigilance.

Writing became fraught. Every sentence was reread, every email second-guessed. Fear of error replaced confidence. Delays were weaponised. Doubt became evidence.

This is how constructive dismissal operates: not through termination, but erosion.

The Compound Effect

The commute was exhausting. The damage came from elsewhere.

The Area of Responsibility stretched from the ACT to the Illawarra. Strategic allocations that would have reduced risk and travel time were denied. Safer routes were reassigned. Longer drives were normalised.

Sunday departures before 1:30 p.m.

Monday circuits through Canberra and Wagga Wagga.

Monthly relocations to short-term accommodation.

Thursday night returns via dead zones and dark roads.

Friday night drives that exceeded four hours, often beginning after 5 p.m.

Near-misses with trucks. Roadkill. Locked brakes. Sliding tyres. Survival mistaken for resilience.

Years Later

Only in conversation with officials from Unions A and C did clarity arrive.

Despite expansive Areas of Responsibility, Regional Organisers were given no allowances for administrative compliance. Credit card acquittals, treated as sackable offences, were required without access to printers, coverage, or time. City-based staff, disconnected from field realities, berated Organisers for failures that were structurally inevitable.

Logic was irrelevant. Control was the point.

The Motto:

Unhappy people will do everything in their power to make others around them equally unhappy.

Tip:

You cannot control how others behave. You can control your response. Give them nothing, and watch the system collapse inward rather than explode onto you.

Union C

Before proceeding, we offer a trigger warning.

The following sequence of events occurred within the first month of employment at Union C.

It involves dangerous working conditions, psychological overload, and exposure to trauma.

It is a true account of:

Ultimate Control

On paper, the role appeared demanding but achievable.

In practice, it was totalising.

The employee from Union C was responsible for an Area of Responsibility that spanned Palm Island, Charters Towers, Ayr, Townsville, and Ingham.

Approximately 175 worksites.

Around 65 Human Resources teams at any given time.

The portfolios were expansive:

Aged Care.

Disability Services.

Health Services, both State and Private.

Local Government.

State Rangers.

Fabrication and industrial sites.

The duties were equally broad.

Be available to work anywhere in the State at short notice.

Prepare briefs and campaigns.

Train and support delegates.

Prepare wage claims.

Attend political functions.

Distribute votes for endorsed candidates at local, state, and federal elections.

Comply with any other task as directed by District, State, Branch, senior officials, or National Office.

The contract was for 40 hours per week.

The reality was closer to 60.

Sometimes more.

This was not framed as excessive.

It was framed as commitment.

As a capability.

As proof you were "up to it."

Control did not present as micromanagement at first.

It presented urgency.

As a moral obligation.

As the quiet implication that saying no meant letting people down.

Within the first month, the employee from Union C was tasked with supporting a member whose partner had died by suicide.

This was not accompanied by clinical support.

There was no debrief.

No adjustment to workload.

No acknowledgement that exposure to acute trauma, layered on top of extreme hours and constant travel, carries risk.

The work continued.

The hours stretched.

The responsibility expanded.

The employee did not yet understand that this was not simply hard work.

It was ultimate control, achieved not through overt threats, but through saturation.

When everything is urgent, nothing is optional.

When everything is your responsibility, nothing is negotiable.

Just Say No

In theory, "no" is a simple word. In practice, it is one of the hardest things to say when the system is built to erode it.

The employee from Union C was conscientious.

Values-driven.

Accustomed to responsibility.

Those traits were not supported.

They were exploited.

Requests were rarely framed as requests.

They were framed as expectations, relayed through tone, timing, and implication.

Declining was not explicitly punished, but it was remembered.

Saying no means explaining yourself.

Explaining yourself meant scrutiny.

Scrutiny meant doubt.

So the no never quite arrived.

Instead, there was adjustment.

Longer days.

Later nights.

More kilometres.

Less rest.

The work did not slow when the employee showed strain.

It accelerated.

This is how control functions in environments that prize output over safety.

You are not ordered to break yourself.

You are given enough rope to do it quietly.

Years Later

It was only years later, in conversation with the employees from Union A and B, who had worked under similar conditions, that clarity arrived.

What had been framed as dedication was, in fact, structural neglect.

What had felt like personal inadequacy was systemic overload.

The employee from Union C came to understand that no role, no matter how important, should place a worker in a position where their own mental health deteriorates to the point of suicidal ideation.

Yet that is exactly what occurred.

The combination of exposure to trauma, excessive workload, constant travel across remote and regional areas, and the absence of protective boundaries created a perfect storm.

By the time the danger was recognised, it had already taken hold.

This is not a failure of resilience. It is the predictable outcome of prolonged, unmitigated pressure.

The Compound Effect

No single task caused the harm.

No single day explains the collapse.

It was the accumulation.

The early mornings.

The late nights.

The relentless responsibility.

The emotional labour.

The kilometres driven.

The trauma was absorbed.

The absence of pause.

Each element, on its own, was survivable.

Together, they were corrosive.

This is the compound effect of excessive workload in roles that conflate commitment with compliance.

Where the worker's humanity becomes secondary to the function they serve.

By the time the cost is visible, it is often profound.

The Motto:

Control does not always shout.

Sometimes it overwhelms until silence feels like relief.

Tip:

If a role requires you to sacrifice your mental health to prove your worth, the role is unsafe, no matter how noble the cause appears.

What becomes clear across Unions A, B, and C is that this was never about capacity, resilience, or dedication.

It was about how systems quietly transfer risk downward, until the moment arrives when someone can no longer carry it.

By then, the conditions that caused the harm have already been normalised, obscured, or reframed.

When the collapse finally comes, it is rarely met with curiosity or accountability. Instead, attention shifts.

Language changes.

Responsibility is redirected.

And the same institutions that engineered the pressure begin to ask a different question altogether, not what happened, but who failed.

That is where the story moves next.

Because once exhaustion, injury, or error appears, the narrative no longer centres on the system that created it.

It centres on the worker who, we are told, has "dropped the ball."

You've Dropped The Ball

THE TERRORIST

The terrorist critiques everything.
When you push back, they weaponise your resistence and declare themselves harmed.

RIGHT WITH YOU

The Terrorist type are people who have superiority complexes.

Easily threatened by anyone who attempts to destabilise their grandiose equilibrium, they then attempt to pull rank, put you in your place and live in hope you second guess yourself.

Left unchecked, this is where Imposter Syndrome either:

Creeps In

(Goal - second guess yourself)

This can be achieved by many means but a common example includes commenting on your contribution at work or online, placing themselves in the role of the expert.

By extension, you are the dimwit. You're not but you are a threat. They can achieve the same sense of insecurity by suggesting they would have handled it differently. Be aware, you didn't necessarily request their feedback or input to begin with, but that is irrelevant. Grandiosity is key here.

Kicks you off your Pedestal

(Goal - destroy self confidence)

This can be achieved in many forms, one of which is the Annual Performance Review (APR).

The review is intended to provide constructive criticism as well as opportunities for areas of improvement, within training objectives identified for the next twelve months.

The current way the APR is handled seems to be a one way process, where feedback is provided on your work output in the previous twelve months.

It does not provide for the employee to offer feedback in return.

The APR process brings about a great deal of stress and pressure on the employee and they feel their work is being picked apart.

Another method for kicking you off your pedestal involves verbal critical communication which may be directed at the way you carry yourself, what you choose to wear, or even your hair colour.

In years past, skin ink has been a bone of contention for an employer. However, these days it doesn't seem to be a huge issue.

This is a welcome change in the cultural aspects of discrimination in the workplace.

What does it matter if one has a tattoo on their arm? Likewise, if someone wants to change their hair colour Blonde to Red, why would it become an issue for a manager to even suggest that the employee change their hair colour back?

Crushes your Soul

(Goal - crazy making)

You are run around in

You never stop

The anticipation of the hit

Constantly thinking ahead for what could go wrong

Preempting what could go wrong

Working ways around it whilst you wait for the hit

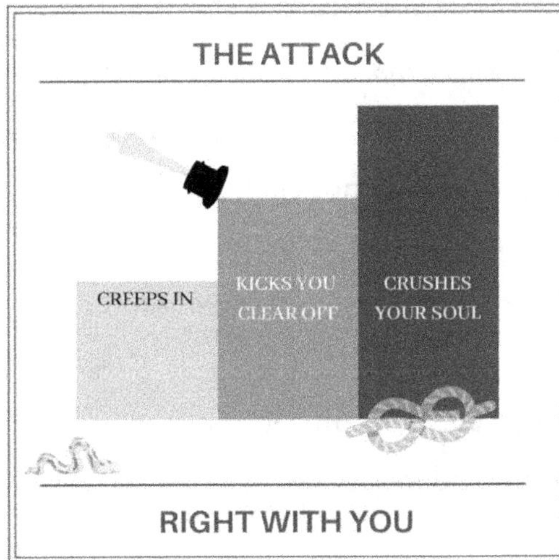

To demonstrate what we are referring to, the following accounts are not anecdotal.

They are real examples of how overload creates mistakes and leads to "performance issues."

Union A

Responsibility Without Authority

The employee from Union A was sent into negotiations with a large regional public-sector employer. On paper, her role was straightforward: represent members, manage negotiations, and deliver outcomes.

In reality, she was placed inside a process already constrained.

Key parameters had been set elsewhere. Political considerations shaped the employer's position. Authority was fragmented across layers the employee from Union A did not control, yet accountability was concentrated squarely on her.

She was the negotiator in the room.

The visible representative.

The person expected to absorb frustration, hostility, and deadlock.

Support from above was implied rather than operational.

Direction shifted depending on the audience.

What was privately acknowledged as difficult was publicly framed as manageable.

At the same time, the organisation knowingly increased her psychological load.

The employee from Union A had disclosed a domestic and family violence situation.

This was not incidental information. It was known, documented, and understood.

Despite this, she was directed to lead a high-profile Domestic and Family Violence campaign.

The campaign's message was urgent and uncompromising.

Its emotional content was sustained and intense.

Its central theme: ***We Won't Wait.***

The work required continuous exposure to trauma narratives, survivor advocacy, public messaging, and media engagement.

All while negotiations with the employer escalated in volatility.

These were not separate pressures.

They were concurrent.

The employee from Union A prepared thoroughly.

She showed up.

She carried negotiations and campaign responsibilities simultaneously, managing conflict on one front while absorbing trauma on the other.

When negotiations diverted, not because of mismanagement, but because the employer pivoted, and the narrative shifted.

Quietly at first.

Then decisively.

Structural constraints disappeared from the story.

Political realities vanished.

What remained was a simplified conclusion: the negotiator had lost control.

She had "dropped the ball."

Just Say No

The employee from Union A pushed back.

She named what was actually occurring: that progress required decisions beyond her authority, that the employer's position was entrenched, and that the cumulative load being placed upon her carried risk.

She refused to perform consensus theatre.

She would not reframe inevitability as personal failure.

That refusal was not treated as professional judgement.

It was recorded as resistance.

The Compound Effect

Once the label landed, everything else reorganised around it.

Fatigue became poor judgement.

Emotional strain became unstable.

Complex negotiations became incompetence.

The Domestic and Family Violence campaign, assigned with full knowledge of her circumstances, was never acknowledged as contributing context. Exposure was separated from outcome. Pressure was denied.

This is how systems protect themselves.

They apply strain, deny its impact, then isolate a visible moment of difficulty and call it failure.

The employee from Union A became the explanation for outcomes that were foreseeable and structurally produced.

Years Later

Years later, the clarity is unavoidable.

There is a long-established principle in law: if you know a person has a pre-existing vulnerability, you remain fully responsible for the harm you cause.

Foreseeable harm does not disappear because it was inconvenient.

Employers sometimes defend this conduct by pointing to uniform treatment, arguing that the role was demanding for everyone, that expectations were consistent, or that others appeared to cope.

But equal exposure is not equal care.

Once vulnerability is known, continuing to apply pressure without adjustment is not neutrality; it is choice.

The law does not reward indifference dressed up as fairness.

The employer did not create the original trauma.

But they knowingly increased exposure.

They layered responsibility without protection.

They assigned visibility without authority.

When strain inevitably appeared, it was reframed as personal failure.

She was not positioned to succeed.

She was positioned to absorb fallout.

The Motto:

Responsibility without authority is not leadership; it is exposure.

Tip:

If an organisation knows your circumstances and increases pressure anyway, stop and reassess.

That is not trust. It is risk being transferred.

Union B

Answer the Goddamn Phone

The authors of this book worked in the realm of reality and opportunity, empowering workers to advocate for themselves in performance processes that were meant to support growth, not destroy it.

Union employees are, of course, subject to performance reviews as well.

The employee from Union B had only one.

As outlined in the previous chapter, it was not a review designed to improve performance.

It was a control mechanism, born of obsession and jealousy, enforced by a Chief of Staff whose fixation crossed the threshold into sexual harassment.

Meetings with male colleagues were monitored. Interactions were scrutinised. The employee's movements and conversations were watched, not for work quality, but for ownership.

That story belongs in Chapter 3.

This chapter begins after the employee from Union B was forced to resign.

What followed was a real-world demonstration of how the phrase "you've dropped the ball" is manufactured.

The employee from Union B was supporting an Associate at a top-tier law firm; one still ranked among Australia's elite.

The Associate had become the subject of a Performance Improvement Plan (PIP), allegedly due to poor output.

From the outset, the process was incoherent.

Multiple partners were involved. Reporting lines shifted. Expectations changed without notice. Eventually, one partner: volatile, domineering, and increasingly aggressive, was assigned as the sole point of contact.

The pandemic arrived.

Work moved home.

Control did not loosen. It intensified.

Emails arrived in the early hours of the morning. Calls followed.

When the Associate silenced her phone overnight to sleep, she began missing calls during the day. She returned them promptly. They went unanswered.

When contact was finally made, the response was explosive:

"When I call, you need to answer the goddamn phone."

Evidence was irrelevant. Call logs, screenshots, timestamps - all dismissed. The narrative had already shifted. What had been framed as performance concerns now included attitude.

Hierarchy was invoked.

"I'm the Partner. You're just an Associate."

From that moment, the Associate was no longer being assessed. She was being managed out.

Just Say No

The Associate eventually set a boundary.

Not a dramatic one. Not a refusal to work. Simply a limit.

A scheduled call was delayed. A bathroom break was taken. A lunch was made.

The phone was not in her hand.

The reaction was immediate and punitive.

A verbal barrage followed, delivered with such speed and aggression that comprehension became impossible. The support person, the former employee from Union B, was dialled in silently as a witness.

The instruction, sent repeatedly via chat, was simple:

End the call. Name the abuse. Protect yourself.

The call ended.

The Associate was stunned.

"He's a Partner. He's meant to be professional."

The response was immediate and accurate.

"I can believe it. You made a fatal error. You said no."

The Compound Effect

From there, everything was reframed.

Missed calls became insubordination.

Unpaid lunch breaks became truancy.

Exercise became misconduct.

Silence became negligence.

The partner began calling at predictable times, ensuring missed calls could be logged.

The Associate was accused of long lunches, misuse of time, and eventually, implied intoxication; based solely on the knowledge that she had once attended a dinner where wine was served.

Each accusation stacked neatly atop the last.

Performance.

Attitude.

Reliability.

Judgement.

Context disappeared.

Output collapsed, not because of incompetence, but because fear replaced cognition. Public humiliation ensured isolation. Colleagues distanced themselves. Invitations stopped. Networking ceased.

The Associate became alone.

And once alone, expendable.

Years Later

Years later, supporting that Associate made something painfully clear.

Evidence does not protect you when a system is invested in your failure.

Screenshots did not matter. Records did not matter. Truth did not matter.

What mattered was that a boundary had been set, hierarchy challenged, and compliance interrupted.

That experience helped the employee from Union B recognise the same pattern at work in the history of the employee from Union A.

Different institutions.

Different roles.

Same mechanism.

A person is overloaded, destabilised, isolated, and then blamed for collapsing under conditions designed to produce that outcome.

The Motto:

In hindsight, everything is 20/20.

Tip:

If you see the pattern forming, do not wait to prove your worth.

You are not being assessed. You are being set up.

Get out before the damage compounds.

Union C

Danger During Probation

The employee from Union C commenced employment with a large industrial organisation and entered a six-month probationary period.

From the outset, his Area of Responsibility was extreme; geographically vast, emotionally demanding, and operationally unsafe.

Within the first month, he was exposed to serious trauma, including direct involvement in matters involving suicide and death. There was no staged induction, no psychological containment, and no structured debrief. The expectation was immediate capacity.

At the same time, the workplace itself became unsafe.

While still within probation, a fellow Organiser accessed the employee from Union C's work-issued computer without his knowledge or consent while he briefly left his desk. An email was sent from his account, impersonating him, to a solicitor external to the organisation, of a personal and inappropriate nature.

This was not addressed as a security breach.

It was not investigated as misconduct.

It was treated as inconsequential.

Weeks later, still within probation, the same colleague used an organisation-issued vehicle to transport a firearm and ammunition to the union office. The weapon and ammunition were placed openly on top of filing cabinets in the shared office space and left unattended while the colleague exited the building.

No formal incident report was made by the employer to external authorities or senior oversight.

No safety protocol was activated.

No risk assessment followed.

Concerns were raised internally. The failure lay in escalation not silence.

The message was implicit: this environment was normal, and tolerance was expected.

Shortly thereafter, explicit sexual material was transmitted to the employee from Union C by the same colleague; graphic content designed to humiliate, intimidate, and offend.

Again, no meaningful intervention occurred.

Then came the threat.

After the employee from Union C noticed a rear door ajar and secured it, inadvertently locking his colleague outside, he was threatened with violence. This occurred while he was still within his probationary period.

One incident crystallised the risk.

A small package was discovered at the front door early one morning. The Organiser raised an immediate concern and suggested to his manager that the police be contacted as a precaution.

That suggestion was rejected.

No external assessment was sought. No safety protocol was triggered. The risk was minimised and absorbed into routine.

This was not uncertainty. It was a decision.

And it occurred while the employee was still within his probationary period.

By this point, the pattern was clear.

Extreme workload.

Uncontained trauma exposure.

Harassment.

Intimidation.

Weapons in the workplace.

All before probation had concluded.

Following the conclusion of probation, USB storage devices belonging to the employee from Union C went missing from his laptop bag. The devices were later observed on the manager's desk.

When questioned, the manager stated that the USBs were his, and suggested that the cleaner may have taken the employee's devices.

No investigation followed.

No audit was conducted.

No data integrity assessment occurred.

The disappearance was treated as incidental, not as a security breach.

Just Say No

There is an expectation, often unspoken, that probationary employees, and other workers in precarious roles, including casuals, will tolerate conditions they should never be exposed to.

Speaking up risks termination.

Silence is framed as professionalism.

The employee from Union C did not have the luxury of refusal.

He continued to perform his duties.

He continued to show up.

He absorbed danger as part of the job because that was the culture being enforced.

The absence of intervention communicated a simple rule: survival was his responsibility alone.

The Compound Effect

Trauma is cumulative.

Unprocessed exposure to death.

Persistent hypervigilance.

Workplace intimidation.

Threats of violence.

Combined with long hours, isolation, and responsibility for vast portfolios, the psychological load became unsustainable.

When the employee from Union C later showed signs of distress, the framing shifted.

The conditions disappeared from view.

The danger was minimised.

What remained was a familiar conclusion:

He couldn't cope.

He dropped the ball.

The same system that ignored risk during probation now used the consequences of that risk as justification.

Years Later

Years later, the clarity is stark.

None of these events were unforeseeable.

None were isolated.

All occurred while the employer retained full control and a heightened duty of care.

Probation did not reduce responsibility.

It increased it.

The employee from Union C was not assessed for resilience.

He was tested by exposure.

And when that exposure caused harm, the narrative was rewritten as personal failure.

The Motto:

Survival is not a performance metric.

Tip:

If danger, harassment, or intimidation are normalised during probation, document immediately.

A system that tolerates risk early will deny responsibility later.

What these accounts demonstrate is not a series of unfortunate incidents, but a pattern with momentum. Each moment of overload, each ignored warning, each reframed boundary does not stand alone.

They stack. They interact. They change how a person thinks, reacts, sleeps, and survives. By the time the phrase "you've dropped the ball" is spoken aloud, the conditions that made the drop inevitable have already done their work.

The next chapter is not about the moment things fall apart. It is about what happens when pressure is applied repeatedly, predictably, and without relief, until the system can finally point to the damage it created and call it proof.

The Compound Effect

THE PUPPETEER

The puppeteer appears harmless. They withdraw contempt, offer approval, and convert the target into an ally. Trust is the entry point. The damage is delayed.

RIGHT WITH YOU

When Small Harms Become Structural Damage

Nothing breaks all at once.

That is the first lie people are taught about harm; that it must be dramatic to be real.

A single incident. A defining confrontation.

A moment so obvious it demands intervention.

That is not how power operates.

Power works quietly. Incrementally. Through repetition. Through normalisation. Through the steady accumulation of small injuries that, taken individually, appear tolerable, even rational, but together become destructive.

This is the compound effect.

It is not theoretical.

It is not abstract.

It is not accidental.

It is measurable.

And it is devastating.

The Nature of Accumulation

The compound effect is what happens when harm is fragmented.

An unpaid hour here.

A delayed response there.

A raised voice dismissed as stress.

A boundary crossed and reframed as commitment.

Each incident is small enough to excuse.

Small enough to explain away.

Small enough to survive.

That is the design.

No single moment feels decisive enough to challenge.

Each one is contextualised, minimised, or reframed as an unfortunate but temporary deviation.

The system relies on this fragmentation.

It depends on your reasonableness, your patience, your instinct to self-regulate rather than disrupt.

You are encouraged to "pick your battles."

You are praised for being "understanding."

You are rewarded for absorbing impact quietly.

By the time the damage becomes visible, it is already embedded, not just in finances, but in confidence, health, relationships, and identity.

This is not resilience failing.

It is arithmetic.

How Normalisation Does the Work

The most effective systems of harm do not rely on cruelty. They rely on normalisation.

What begins as an exception quickly becomes precedent. What begins as "just this once" becomes expectation. The line does not move suddenly. It shifts incrementally, until you are standing somewhere you never agreed to be.

Over time, you stop noticing what you are giving up:

- time that is no longer yours
- energy that is never restored
- rest that must be justified
- boundaries that require explanation

The body notices before the mind does.

Fatigue becomes background noise. Hyper-vigilance is reframed as professionalism. Anxiety is mislabelled as dedication. You learn to function while depleted, and the system interprets this as capacity.

This is how harm is compounded, not through excess, but through endurance.

Union A

The Original Template

Long before union offices or enterprise bargaining tables, the pattern was learned elsewhere.

In the family business, the employee from Union A occupied the administrative, financial, and managerial nerve centre. The role expanded continuously, not through promotion, training, or renegotiation, but through expectation.

Availability was assumed. Extra hours were invisible. Responsibility was elastic.

High performance did not lead to trust. It triggered a threat. Boundaries were interpreted as defiance. Questions were reframed as disloyalty. Pay discussions were personalised, emotionalised, and ultimately weaponised. What should have been structural conversations were recast as moral ones.

What followed was not a single act of abuse, but a familiar and recognisable sequence:

- Allegations of misconduct, escalating in severity
- False claims regarding financial impropriety
- Denigration of work quality despite consistent output
- Higher duties without training or remuneration
- Withheld opportunities for rest or recovery
- Cyclical conflict with no resolution
- Chronic miscommunication framed as employee failure
- Unreasonable workloads presented as expectation

None of these acts, in isolation, would appear catastrophic. Together, they dismantled trust, stability, and safety.

This was not a conflict.

It was conditioning.

Money Is Never "Just Money"

In workplaces that brand themselves as values-driven, particularly family businesses, and in some cases organisations whose public role is to negotiate wages, money is often treated as an uncomfortable topic.

This framing is not benign.

It is strategic.

Underpayment compounds.

Unpaid hours accumulate quietly.

Superannuation losses multiply invisibly.

Career interruptions narrow future opportunities.

Burnout delays recovery, and earning capacity.

What appears as a marginal discrepancy on a weekly payslip becomes a structural disadvantage over a lifetime.

In the family business, remuneration was framed as generous because it exceeded award rates. What it did not capture were the hours outside ordinary business time, the constant accessibility, the emotional labour, and the absence of any true comparator role.

Above-award pay does not negate exploitation when the scope of work is unlimited.

This was not a family disagreement over money.

It was the first ledger entry in a long-term loss.

What was learned here did not stay here.

The Institutional Echo: When Patterns Scale

What is learned privately is often replicated professionally.

The environment changes.

The language shifts.

The structure looks more legitimate.

The pattern remains.

Union B

The Delegate Who Asked to Be Consulted

At Union B, the compound effect did not begin with overt hostility. It began with something far more subtle: the quiet removal of voice.

While working at FSG, the employee from Union B served as a workplace delegate. This was not a self-appointed role, nor was it performative. Delegates exist for a reason: to provide a structured conduit between workers and management, particularly when change is proposed or imposed.

The requests made were modest.

The expectations were reasonable.

The obligation already existed.

Workers wanted to be consulted about changes that directly affected their work, safety, and conditions.

Consultation is not an abstract principle. It is a practical safeguard embedded in employment law and industrial instruments precisely because unilateral decision-making creates risk. It is designed to slow things down. To force consideration. To interrupt impulse, ego, and expediency.

At FSG, consultation was treated as optional.

Decisions were made behind closed doors and communicated after the fact. Workers were informed, not engaged. When concerns were raised, they were reframed as resistance rather than participation. The delegate's role was tolerated only so long as it remained symbolic; a title without teeth.

This is how the compound effect takes hold at an organisational level: when processes exist on paper, but quietly stripped of consequence.

When the delegate asserted the obligation to consult, not as a threat, but as a reminder, the response was immediate and telling.

The Human Resources manager reacted with visible anger.

Not confusion.

Not disagreement.

Anger.

Because consultation, properly applied, disrupts control. It demands justification. It creates witnesses. It limits discretion. For those accustomed to unilateral authority, it feels like insubordination, even when it is lawful, reasonable, and required.

From that point on, the environment shifted.

The delegate was scrutinised.

Workers who spoke up were watched more closely.

Minor issues were elevated.

Discipline replaced dialogue.

The message was clear, even if it was never articulated: participation came at a cost.

Eventually, after escalation beyond the immediate workplace, the Human Resources manager was demoted. The outcome confirmed what the workers had known all along: the employer had been legally obliged to consult. The delegate had not overstepped. The process had been breached.

But by then, the damage was entrenched.

The absence of genuine consultation had allowed poor governance to take root. Decisions went unchallenged. Vulnerable workers, particularly those with limited job security or bargaining power, were targeted for minor indiscretions. Fear replaced trust. Silence replaced engagement.

What followed was not sudden collapse, but gradual decay.

At FSG, unresolved governance failures compounded. Oversight weakened. Accountability eroded. Eventually, corruption went unnoticed or unaddressed. The organisation entered receivership, leaving more than 900 employees suddenly without work.

The workers did not fail the system.

The system failed, because it refused to listen to its workers.

This is the cost of treating consultation as inconvenient rather than essential. It is not merely a procedural breach; it is an accelerant. When workers are excluded from decisions that affect them, small governance failures multiply unchecked, until the consequences can no longer be contained.

That is the compound effect at scale.

Union C

Tokens Instead of Time, Surveillance Instead of Support

At Union C, the compound effect was not delivered in a single act of deprivation. It arrived through a series of decisions that, on paper, appeared minor, reasonable, and defensible, but in practice accumulated into something far more dangerous.

The $50 gift cards issued to administrative staff were emblematic, not exceptional.

Instead of a wage increase that would compound over time - lifting base pay, superannuation, leave accruals, and future bargaining positions - administrative staff were given a token reward. A gesture framed as appreciation. A one-off designed to feel generous without creating obligation.

The arithmetic was clear.

A gift card is spent once, and then disappears.

A percentage wage increase compounds every pay cycle, every year.

One creates a moment. The other creates security.

The decision to substitute the former for the latter was not neutral. It locked in long-term disadvantage while allowing leadership to perform gratitude. Appreciation became theatrical. Structural equity was deferred, indefinitely.

But the gift cards were only one layer.

What followed was not a single failure, but a cascade: economic, temporal, psychological, and organisational.

Workload Without Limits

For the employee from Union C, responsibility was not merely expanded, it was saturated.

The Area of Responsibility spanned vast geographic distances, encompassing regional and remote locations that required constant travel, long hours, and sustained vigilance. The workload was relentless, but it was framed as necessity rather than choice.

Travel was not treated as labour.

Recovery was not treated as essential.

Risk was normalised.

Sunday departures bled into Monday circuits.

Thursday nights ended on dark roads.

Friday returns occurred long after exhaustion set in.

Near-misses were shrugged off.

Fatigue was reframed as resilience.

No single journey was deemed unsafe enough to challenge. No individual week was extreme enough to justify intervention. The danger lay in the accumulation: the miles driven while depleted, the decisions made while cognitively taxed, the body absorbing risk long after judgement was compromised.

This is how the compound effect functions in operational roles, not by asking too much at once, but by asking too much for too long.

Time Was Never Neutral

At Union C, time itself became a mechanism of harm.

Travel time was treated as incidental rather than occupational.

Long drives across regional and remote Queensland were absorbed into the working week without recalibration of workload, rest, or safety expectations.

Preparation, recovery, and decompression were invisible.

This mattered.

Time spent driving while exhausted is not neutral.

Time spent away from home erodes relationships, routine, and recovery. Time spent "on call" - mentally or emotionally - is still labour, even when it is not recorded.

Yet each extension of time was justified as temporary.

Each sacrifice was framed as situational.

Each overreach was normalised by precedent.

The organisation benefited from constant coverage and responsiveness while the cost: fatigue, isolation, cognitive load, was carried privately.

This is how time compounds into harm, not through a single demand, but through the steady conversion of personal hours into an institutional asset.

Trauma as Task, Not Risk

Within the first month of employment, the employee from Union C was tasked with supporting a member whose partner had died by suicide.

There was no clinical support.

No debrief.

No adjustment to workload.

Exposure to acute trauma was treated as part of the job, rather than a recognised psychological risk. The work did not slow. It accelerated.

This was not resilience-building. It was erosion.

When trauma is layered onto excessive workload and constant travel, the impact compounds rapidly. Each additional responsibility narrows capacity, yet the system interprets continued functioning as consent.

The employee did not yet understand that this was not simply demanding work. It was saturation: a method of control achieved not through overt threat, but through volume.

When everything is urgent, nothing is negotiable.

When everything is your responsibility, nothing is optional.

Role Creep Without Renegotiation

As pressure increased, so did the scope of responsibility, but not through promotion, consultation, or agreement.

The employee from Union C absorbed additional roles quietly: counsellor, crisis responder, mediator, logistics coordinator. None of these were formally acknowledged. None were supported with training or safeguards. None triggered a reassessment of workload or risk.

This was not flexible. It was a silent expansion.

Role creep is one of the most effective compound mechanisms in institutions.

Because it happens gradually, it rarely triggers resistance.

Because it is framed as trust, it feels affirming, at first.

Over time, however, the worker becomes indispensable but unsupported. Accountable without authority. Responsible without protection.

By the time the role becomes unmanageable, it has already been internalised as expectation.

Surveillance and Isolation

As strain became visible, support did not follow.

Instead, scrutiny increased.

Communications were monitored.

Movements were tracked.

Minor administrative issues were elevated.

Surveillance replaced supervision. Isolation replaced assistance.

The employee learned, implicitly, that slowing down would invite suspicion, not care.

That asking for support would be recorded, not addressed.

That vulnerability would be interpreted as weakness.

This is a critical moment in the compound effect: when a system responds to strain not by reducing load, but by tightening control.

Fear does not need to be explicit to be effective. It only needs to be consistent.

When Collapse Is Treated as Surprise

By the time suicidal ideation emerged, the organisation treated it as an unexpected rupture: a sudden and individual crisis.

It was neither.

The warning signs had been present for months: sustained fatigue, emotional saturation, isolation, and escalating scrutiny. Each was visible. Each was contextualised away. Each was absorbed into the narrative of dedication.

This is a defining feature of the compound effect: when systems ignore early indicators and then express shock at the outcome.

Collapse is not sudden when pressure is constant.

It is delayed recognition.

The outcome was an employee in an acute psychological crisis; one who attended the office late on a Friday evening, believing he would not be alive by the following week.

Intervention came NOT from the institution, but by chance: an unexpected message from a friend that disrupted what had become, in his mind, an inevitable conclusion.

At that point, the employee believed his death would finally make visible what he could no longer survive. That the accumulation of bullying, intimidation, and institutional neglect had reached a point where endurance itself felt complicit.

This was not martyrdom. It was the internalisation of systemic failure.

When organisations delay recognition long enough, workers are left to interpret collapse as personal weakness rather than the predictable result of sustained harm.

Economic Harm Meets Psychological Collapse

The $50 gift cards now take on their full meaning.

They sit alongside:

- unpaid and unrecognised labour
- extended travel without adequate safeguards
- exposure to trauma without support
- surveillance masquerading as management
- the absence of structural wage progression

Each element compounds the next.

Lower pay limits recovery options.

Fatigue increases risk.

Trauma narrows perspective.

Surveillance silences dissent.

By the time suicidal ideation emerged, the danger was already embedded. No single decision caused the collapse.

This was not a failure of character.

It was the predictable outcome of prolonged, unmitigated pressure.

Recognition, Too Late

Only years later, in conversation with employees from Unions A and B, did clarity arrive.

What had been framed as dedication was, in fact, structural neglect.

What had felt like personal inadequacy was systemic overload.

The employee from Union C came to understand that no role, no matter how important, should place a worker in a position where their mental health deteriorates to the point of suicidal ideation.

Yet that is exactly what occurred.

This is the compound effect in its most dangerous form: when economic minimisation, workload saturation, and psychological exposure converge; quietly, steadily, and without interruption.

Acknowledgement

The compound effect only works when harm goes unnamed.

Once patterns are identified, their power diminishes. What feels personal becomes structural. What felt like individual failure reveals itself as systemic design.

Nothing here was accidental.

Nothing here was isolated.

The damage was not caused by one decision, one person, or one bad day. It was caused by a system that relies on tolerance, silence, and incremental erosion.

Once seen, it cannot be unseen.

The Psychological Ledger

The most dangerous myth about harm is that it ends when employment ends.

It does not.

Trauma does not operate on HR timelines. It does not respect resignation dates, redundancy letters, or exit interviews.

It waits. It resurfaces. It often emerges years later, when life is otherwise stable, and demands to be accounted for.

The employee from Union A returned to work after only a short break, aware that extended absence would itself be treated as a liability. This decision was pragmatic. It was also costly.

Australian workplaces routinely reward presenteeism while punishing recovery. Working through illness, stress, and injury is normalised, even valorised. The long-term consequences are externalised onto individuals.

Years later, the accumulated impact of earlier harm resurfaced, not because the employee was weak, but because unresolved trauma compounds just as surely as unpaid wages.

The bill does not disappear.

It waits.

Three Unions. One Equation.

By the time the stories of Union A, B, and C are placed side by side, the pattern is no longer subtle. The settings differ. The roles differ. The stated values differ. The mechanism does not.

Across all three unions, harm did not arrive as a single breach or a dramatic event. It arrived through accumulation. Through small decisions that were individually defensible and collectively devastating.

At Union A, unpaid labour, blurred boundaries, and financial ambiguity were normalised under the language of loyalty and flexibility. What began as accommodation became - expectation. What was framed as generosity became leverage.

At Union B, the removal of consultation hollowed out governance from the inside. Workers were excluded from decisions that affected their safety and livelihoods. Process existed, but consequence did not. Silence was mistaken for stability until collapse made that illusion impossible to sustain.

At Union C, economic minimisation, workload saturation, trauma exposure, and surveillance converged. Token rewards replaced structural obligation. Time was extracted without limit. Risk was externalised onto the worker. When the inevitable psychological consequences emerged, they were treated as personal failure rather than organisational design.

None of this required malice.

That is the most confronting truth.

The compound effect does not depend on cruelty. It depends on tolerance. On the quiet agreement to absorb one more demand, one more compromise, one more erosion, because each, on its own, feels survivable.

Institutions rely on this incrementalism.

They rely on the fact that people are more likely to endure gradual harm than resist sudden injustice.

They rely on fragmentation to prevent recognition.

But when these stories are viewed together, the arithmetic becomes undeniable.

Economic harm compounds.

Psychological harm compounds.

Governance failure compounds.

And when no one intervenes early, the cost is paid later.

In burnout, breakdown, collapse, and loss.

The damage was not caused by one person, one decision, or one bad day. It was caused by systems that allowed small harms to accumulate unchecked.

That is the compound effect.

The Motto:

DO NOTHING, NOTHING CHANGES.

Part 2
How Systems Behave

Fish & Chips: Buying Loyalty With Leverage

THE TYRANT

The Tyrant begins quietly. They build leverage before conflict exists and collect obedience before consent is withdrawn.

RIGHT WITH YOU

Behaviour is watched.

Appearance is observed, scrutinised, and commented upon.

Your online activity is monitored.

So begins the cycle of mobbing.

This process is repeated, scaled, and sustained, depending on how many people the Tyrant chooses to send after you.

When you are living your life outside of work, your actual life, it is suddenly recast as evidence.

You are out too much. You drink too much. You must be a "lady who lunches" or some kind of "gay creative."

These narratives are not observations. They are instruments.

Now, before we go any further, let us be clear: that baggage is not yours. We will not project our experience onto you.

What is happening here is not curiosity. It is surveillance dressed up as concern.

It is crucial, and we cannot state this enough, to recognise the following universal truths:

- A workplace bully, once committed to bullying, will not stop to reflect on their behaviour
- The Tyrant observes their target, identifies a perceived vulnerability, and uses it
- The initial trigger is often unconscious and emotive
- They are unaware that their own insecurity has been activated
- Rather than pause and reflect, they react
- What follows is conscious, deliberate behaviour designed to neutralise or destroy you

With this type of character, the more you challenge, the less likely resolution becomes.

This is not accidental. It is a tactic. One designed to keep you trapped in a cycle where you are branded the "troublemaker" for refusing to absorb harm quietly.

As challenges escalate, employers or managers may become flustered and begin to lie, not always boldly, but strategically; to protect themselves.

These lies often surface after formal processes have concluded, when the opportunity to respond has passed.

They are targeted. They are personal. And they are among the most difficult to process.

This is where a fundamental principle of employment law becomes relevant:

The Right of Reply

It is important to understand the character you are dealing with in this chapter.

These individuals are unreliable, evade responsibility, and yet demand loyalty. When loyalty cannot be secured through trust or integrity, it is extracted through leverage.

We will explore this further in the next chapter, through the corporate psychopath's unspoken creed:

If I go down, you all go down.

This is a layered process. Not in relation to your feelings or needs, those are routinely disregarded, but in relation to the characters involved and the roles they play.

You may have a long-standing working relationship with a colleague, someone you once trusted.

That colleague may step into a managerial role in pursuit of status or power. Others may move into similar roles and become instruments of management without fully realising it.

When conflict arises, you find yourself in an impossible position: laughing along to survive, or standing alone.

Either way, the isolation is the point.

It is worth pausing here for one reason only: to make something explicit.

The perpetrators are the problem.

Not the victim.

At the time, however, this was almost impossible to see.

The victim's attention is consumed by deciphering the code: analysing tone, interpreting subtext, assessing motive, and constantly recalibrating what is real and what is not.

The cognitive load is relentless.

Clarity is crowded out by survival.

It is only later, often with distance, that the pattern becomes visible.

What emerges is not complexity, but predictability.

The perpetrators are not misunderstood.

They are:

- incompetent,
- lazy,
- actively sabotaging,
- detached from reality, and
- convinced that everything revolves around them.

In short, it is their way or the highway.

Once leverage is in place, the system no longer needs your agreement, only your silence.

Union A

I'm So Sick of This

It began with sick leave.

Or rather, that is what it was labelled.

The employee continued to attend work, often while unwell. On multiple occasions, they arrived, attempted to push through the day, and then had to leave partway through, because their health deteriorated. This was visible. Nothing was hidden.

Colleagues did ask whether the employee was okay.

What became clear over time, however, was that this concern was not neutral. It was condescending. It was managerial. And it functioned less as support than as observation.

The employee was open about their circumstances. Too open, in hindsight. At the time, it felt reasonable to trust colleagues with the reality of their life. They were carrying an extraordinary load, including supporting a daughter who was suicidal. There were days the employee attended work already in distress, crying on colleagues' shoulders, not concealing their vulnerability, and not seeking special treatment.

That openness was later used against them.

The information shared, about health, family, and emotional strain, did not remain where it was offered. It travelled. It was interpreted. It was repurposed.

The operative question was no longer:

Are you okay?

It became:

How much can you carry and still comply?

Surveillance Disguised as Concern

What followed was not disciplinary action. It did not need to be.

Instead, it unfolded through group behaviour.

Supportive conversations became referential.

Check-ins became data points.

Care became commentary.

The employee was observed, not because others feared they might fall, but because the organisation was assessing how much pressure could be applied before something gave way.

This is how mobbing begins, not with overt hostility, but with proximity, access, and information gathered under the guise of care.

No single act was cruel. That is what makes it difficult to name.

Together, however, these acts formed a pattern: a collective tightening in which concern flowed upward and judgement flowed back down.

Sick Leave as Leverage

At a certain point, sick leave ceased to be personal leave.

It became a narrative.

Not because the employee was absent, but because they were visibly struggling in a workplace that would later treat vulnerability as a liability.

Patterns were inferred. Motives quietly assigned. Credibility subtly eroded.

Systems designed to protect workers are often defended by pointing out that they can be misused. That claim is familiar. It is frequently invoked.

But this was not an instance of avoidance or opportunism.

The employee continued to attend work while unwell. They attempted to meet their obligations. Their deterioration was visible, documented, and contextual. What emerged was not a pattern of absence, but a pattern of decline.

That distinction mattered. And it was deliberately erased.

By reframing legitimate illness as manipulation, and openness as unreliability, care was collapsed into suspicion.

What should have prompted support instead became justification for surveillance, judgement, and control.

What mattered was not whether the employee was meeting their obligations.

What mattered was whether their vulnerability could be repurposed as leverage.

This reframing did not arise from policy.

It arose from permission.

Once a leader signals, directly or indirectly, that someone is a problem, others adjust accordingly, not out of malice, but self-preservation.

This is how group violence embeds itself.

Regain Control

There is a moment in every mobbing process when the target is expected to submit, not explicitly, but psychologically.

To accept the framing.

To internalise the doubt.

To apologise for existing.

The employee did not.

They questioned the narrative.

They asserted their reality.

They resisted the quiet expectation of gratitude for treatment framed as concern.

That resistance marked the turning point.

Concern hardened into irritation. Support evaporated.

What had been framed as care revealed itself as conditional compliance.

This is the pivot point in mobbing:

When care becomes conditional, and obedience is mistaken for cooperation.

Just Say No

Saying no was interpreted as defiance.

Not because it disrupted work, but because it disrupted the story being constructed.

Once a group settles on a version of events, truth becomes inconvenient. Boundaries are reframed as an attitude. Resistance becomes insubordination.

From that point on, the employee's actions were filtered through a predetermined lens.

The Compound Effect

None of what occurred was catastrophic in isolation.

That is precisely how it survived scrutiny.

Instead, the harm accumulated:

- altered tone
- subtle exclusions
- raised eyebrows
- strategic silences
- the slow rewriting of the employee's character

By the time formal processes appeared, the outcome had already been decided socially.

The paperwork simply followed.

This is the compound effect of mobbing.

Years Later

With distance, the pattern became unmistakable.

This was never about sick leave.

It was never about policy.

It was never about performance.

It was about control exercised collectively, with sufficient diffused responsibility to keep everyone comfortable.

That is what makes mobbing so difficult to articulate and so easy to deny.

There is no single incident to point to, only a pattern that becomes visible once the target is no longer inside it.

By then, the damage has already been done.

Union B

Too Much Control

By the time the employee from Union B understood what was happening, her life had already been reorganised around control, exercised through exhaustion.

Not metaphorically. Literally.

Every Sunday followed the same ritual: self-defence training in the morning, packing in the afternoon, then a long drive south. Hotels. Hospitals. Corridors.

Meetings that bled into nights. Mornings that arrived without sleep. Weeks without rest. A body running on adrenaline and duty long after it should have stopped.

At the time, she believed this was commitment. She believed this was leadership. She believed this was what solidarity demanded. She did not yet understand that she was being slowly displaced from her own centre of gravity.

How It Started

Before the travel grind, before the packed bags, there was a shift in tone.

Once viewed as capable, resilient, dependable, the employee from Union B was suddenly left to work it out for herself. Requests for guidance went unanswered. Calls were ignored or deflected. Support was conditional, erratic, or deliberately withheld. Advice, when it came, was dismissive, incorrect, or weaponised later to assign blame.

"We never had this problem before."

"We never needed to have a policy on this issue before you came along."

This was not said as a reflection. It was said as an indictment.

This was not random. It was patterned.

A manager became unavailable. An Industrial Officer became adversarial. Responsibility flowed downward without authority flowing with it. Critical decisions were forced onto her, then retrospectively criticised. Mistakes, real or manufactured, were used to justify more scrutiny, more control, more isolation.

The work itself became impossible to complete safely.

But the message was clear: cope anyway.

The Group Closes In

Group violence rarely announces itself.

It emerges through alignment.

Emails that include everyone except you. Meetings where your name is spoken but your presence is unnecessary. Inside jokes that land as silences. Eye contact withheld. Instructions contradicted. Allies quietly stepping back.

When she raised concerns, she was told to "ignore it." When she asked for clarity, she was accused of attitude. When she drew boundaries, she was framed as difficult. When she became visibly unwell, the response was not care, but inconvenience.

No one asked in a way that changed anything.

The unspoken question was always: Are you loyal?

Loyalty, in this environment, meant silence. It meant absorbing abuse without naming it. It meant carrying risk without complaint. It meant performing competence while being structurally undermined.

And when she persisted, the language shifted again.

"Just leave it be."

"You've already done enough damage."

Damage, in this context, meant only one thing:

The employee from Union B doing what she was employed to do.

Her job.

The Illusion of Support

There were moments that looked like intervention.

A restructure. A new reporting line. A meeting framed as resolution. A promise that "things will improve."

They never did.

Because the same people remained. The same behaviours persisted. The same informal power structures were held.

At times, she was positioned between senior figures who openly disliked one another, expected to mediate their conflict while maintaining obedience to both.

At other times, she was tasked with managing suicidal workers without policy guidance, legal backing, or emotional support. Then criticised for how she handled the aftermath.

When she sought external advice, she was told to keep it internal.

When she prioritised safety, she was accused of overreacting.

When she documented incidents, she was framed as building a case.

The mob does not need unanimity.

It only needs enough people to look away.

The Cost

The impact was cumulative.

Sleep fractured. Appetite disappeared. The phone became a source of dread. Travel became dangerous. The body began to fail under sustained stress. Relationships frayed. Identity narrowed to survival.

She lost volunteer roles. She stopped exercising. She stopped resting. She stopped imagining a future beyond the next demand.

At one point, driving exhausted on dark roads, she caught herself thinking that crashing would at least mean rest.

That moment mattered.

Because it marked the point where the body recognised what the mind had not yet accepted: this was no longer work. It was harmful.

Just Say No

The turning point did not come with validation or apology. It came with refusal.

Refusing after-hours contact. Refusing unsafe directives. Refusing to absorb emotional labour without authority. Refusing to pretend this was normal.

Each boundary triggered backlash. Each assertion of autonomy was met with escalation. But something else happened too: the spell weakened.

The narrative that she was the problem no longer held.

Others had experienced the same treatment. Others had been burned out, sidelined, or pushed out. Others had learned that survival required silence, or exit.

The Compound Effect

None of this happened in a single incident.

It happened through accumulation.

One ignored call. One misdirected task. One unsafe demand. One public undermining. One private threat. One night without sleep. One more drive. One more crisis.

Over time, the employee from Union B was no longer functioning within the organisation.

She was being consumed by it.

Years Later

Only with distance did the pattern become unmistakable.

The perpetrators were not overworked heroes.

They were disorganised, inconsistent, and protected.

They relied on chaos.

They mistook authority for entitlement.

They interpreted resistance as betrayal.

Most of all, they believed the system existed to serve them.

The group violence was not accidental. It was structural.

And walking away, though costly, was the first act of recovery.

Union C

I'm In Control Here, Not You

If you want to understand how mobbing survives scrutiny, start here:

He said, she said.

Every single one of these matters can be reduced to that core attribute.

And once the narrative is framed that way, the system stops looking for truth and starts looking for balance.

It becomes less about what happened, and more about whose version feels safer to accept.

"He said, she said" cases are the hardest to crack for four reasons:

- There are two parties affected, each with conflicting accounts.
- There is an external reviewer: investigator, insurer, regulator - positioned as neutral.
- That reviewer is not a blank slate. They bring their own biases, assumptions, and sometimes lived experience that shapes what they consider "credible."
- The bully will lie without fear of retribution, and without blinking.

All of this unfolds inside a cultural myth that still dominates how people interpret harm:

A Fair & Just World.

In a fair and just world, bad things only happen to bad people. So if you're being targeted, the listener's brain tries to resolve the discomfort by turning the spotlight back onto you:

Maybe you're the problem.

Maybe you lack insight. Maybe your story doesn't add up.

And when the idea of a victim is too confronting, the default response becomes discrediting, and disguised as concern:

- Maybe if you'd left sooner, things would be different.
- Maybe if you'd spoken out, they might have stopped.
- Maybe they didn't realise what they said hurt you.
- Maybe if you'd played nicer, this would have ended differently.
- Maybe you're not cut out for this job.

These statements often arrive in the form of "questions," but they aren't questions. They are qualifiers: sentences designed to shrink your credibility without taking responsibility for doubting you.

So let's name it plainly:

We live in a victim-full society that still shames the victim, while insisting it believes in fairness and justice.

If you were treated badly, the story must be that you deserved it, or caused it, or failed to prevent it.

Fun times.

Now let's bring it back to what this looks like in practice.

The Example:

The Lie That Lands After the Process.

This is where mobbing gets clever.

It isn't only bullying that harms.

It's the administrative afterlife of bullying: the version of events that gets lodged, repeated, and accepted once the worker no longer has equal access to reply.

This is where the worker discovers what power really sounds like:

You don't get to tell your story.

You only get to respond to theirs.

Just Say No

Saying "no" in a "he said / she said" environment isn't a simple boundary.

It becomes a risk.

Not because you are wrong, but because the system is designed to interpret boundaries as attitude, and discomfort as instability.

The moment you push back, you are no longer framed as a worker raising concerns.

You are framed as a problem to manage.

The Compound Effect

The dangerous part is that none of these lies land as a single catastrophic event. They land as small distortions:

- a casual omission
- a "misunderstanding" written down as fact
- a timeline shifted
- a motive attributed
- a witness not contacted
- a call "attempted" that never occurred
- an "independent" conclusion reached before all evidence is gathered

Each one is survivable. Each one is deniable. Together, they create the outcome: confusion, self-doubt, and erosion of credibility. That is the compound effect of narrative control.

And that is why the victim starts asking the most dangerous question of all: What if I really am the problem?

What to Do Instead

To survive this kind of system, you have to become what mobbing fears most:

Meticulous.

Not emotional.

Not performative.

Not apologetic.

Meticulous.

- Pick apart statements without apology.
- Document sequences, not just incidents.
- Track decision points: who decided, who approved, who benefited.
- Keep records that outlast tone, reputation, and fatigue.
- Be clear about your intention: accuracy.

Because when the system relies on forgetting, records become "resistance." This is not advice. It is what remains when truth is no longer enough.

The Devil in the Detail

What "he said / she said" actually looks like is this: A series of witness statements submitted years after the events, each containing small but consequential distortions: dates moved, conversations reimagined, roles reframed, complaints minimised, and responsibility displaced. None of the statements collapse under scrutiny on their own. That is the point. Instead, the worker is forced into an impossible position: rebutting assertions they never made, meetings that never occurred, timelines that don't align, and claims of "no complaint received", despite evidence to the contrary. Each response requires forensic attention:

- correcting dates, identifying who was present, and who was not
- pointing out contradictions between statements
- challenging assertions made without contemporaneous records
- explaining why complaints stopped being raised after confidentiality was breached

This is not truth-seeking. It is attrition by paperwork.

The burden quietly shifts.

The bully does not need to prove anything.

The worker must disprove everything.

The more time the worker spends defending the details, because that is where the devil lies, the more exhausted they become. Attention narrows. Energy drains. Perspective collapses. Slowly, almost imperceptibly, they lose sight of why the process began at all. And why did it begin? Because the worker was psychologically injured by their place of employment, by the people in it, by what was done to them, and by what was not done when intervention was required.

That truth is gradually buried beneath dates, footnotes, rebuttals, and administrative distraction. And the further away from the original events the process moves, the easier it becomes for decision-makers to say, “It’s difficult to know what really happened.”

That uncertainty is not a flaw in the system. It is the system working exactly as designed.

(The full set of annotated witness statements provided to the insurer illustrates this pattern in granular detail.)

Years Later

It is usually years later that clarity arrives, not because you were naïve, but because you were overloaded. Inside the storm, you’re trying to function. Outside the storm, you can finally see the pattern:

It was never “he said / she said.”

It was power said.

And the system listened.

Across Union A, Union B, and Union C, the differences in circumstance are superficial.

The pattern is not.

In each case, control is exercised first through proximity and pressure, then through narrative and compliance, and finally through collective behaviour that isolates the target while preserving plausible deniability.

What appears, on the surface, as individual conflict, workload pressure, or administrative misunderstanding is, in practice, the same mechanism operating in different forms.

The outcome is predictable:

exhaustion,

confusion,

self-doubt, and

silence.

This is how mobbing sustains itself, not through chaos, but through coordination that never needs to be acknowledged. And once enough people have been drawn into protecting the system rather than the worker, the rules change.

Loyalty is no longer requested.

It is enforced.

That is where the next chapter begins.

If I Go Down, You All Go Down

THE DICTATOR

The Dictator rules by ultimatum.
Compliance is rewarded.
Resistence is punished.
If they fall, they take others with them.

RIGHT WITH YOU

The standard you walk past is the standard you accept.

In functional workplaces, authority is exercised through policy, process, and accountability.

Power is meant to be constrained by rules, transparency, and consequence.

In dysfunctional workplaces, authority operates differently.

It is not governed by systems, but by fear.

This chapter examines the environment in which power is maintained through collective consequence, where one person's dissent becomes everyone's risk.

In these settings, silence is not merely encouraged; it is enforced.

Loyalty is not something built through trust or shared purpose, but something extracted through intimidation, reward, and threat.

The Dictator does not need to say the words out loud.

If I go down, you all go down is rarely spoken, yet it is always understood.

This chapter is not about ego, personality clashes, or individual bad actors acting in isolation.

It is about a recurring pattern of authoritarian control that emerges when accountability fails and institutions prioritise stability over truth.

The crime does not fit the time.

But the punishment is designed to be visible.

The Dictator

The Dictator is often misunderstood.

They are rarely chaotic, and they are not always openly aggressive.

More often, they are strategic, composed, and outwardly reasonable.

They may present as blunt but honest, demanding but fair, decisive rather than cruel.

Their power lies not in volatility, but in certainty.

They understand something fundamental about institutional behaviour: most people will tolerate harm, compromise values, and remain silent if the alternative is becoming the next target.

The Dictator does not rely on universal agreement, only on widespread fear.

Control is maintained through implication.

Consequences are not always spelled out.

They are inferred.

A single public example is enough to establish the rules.

Once established, those rules are self-policing.

The Dictator governs through three interlocking mechanisms:

Collective consequence: one person's resistance becomes everyone's exposure

Transactional loyalty: allegiance is bought, traded, or coerced

Moral inversion: integrity is reframed as disloyalty or disruption

In this environment, compliance is framed as professionalism. Silence becomes maturity. Survival is mistaken for loyalty.

Why Genuine People Are Targeted

It is a common assumption that those targeted by Dictators are weak, naïve, or incapable of navigating workplace politics. The reality is the opposite. The people targeted in these environments are often principled, values-driven, and sincere. They ask questions. They notice inconsistencies. They take stated values seriously. They believe process should mean something. This is precisely why they are dangerous.

Genuine people disrupt systems built on performance and pretense. They do not instinctively play along with moral shortcuts or strategic silence. Their presence introduces friction into environments that depend on unspoken agreements.

The Dictator does not fear incompetence.

They fear clarity.

Demonstration One: Public Humiliation

Public humiliation is not an emotional outburst. It is a tactic: one designed to be witnessed.

At Union A, the employee had built a reputation for diligence and reliability. She was known for carrying heavy workloads and absorbing pressure without complaint. When she raised concerns about unreasonable expectations and unsafe practices, the response was not discussion or correction. Instead, her competence was quietly undermined.

Meetings occurred without her. Decisions were made and attributed to her without consultation. Eventually, criticism that had never been raised privately appeared suddenly, fully formed, and disproportionate. When the humiliation arrived, it did not look like shouting. It looked like credibility being stripped in plain sight.

The message was subtle but unmistakable: this is what happens when you question the way things are done.

At Union B, the humiliation was more overt. A minor administrative issue, one that would normally be resolved informally, became a public spectacle. A worker was dismissed in front of others, not because the error was significant, but because the moment was useful. The Dictator did not correct behaviour. They established dominance.

Observers learned quickly. It was not the mistake that mattered. It was who made it, and what they had previously challenged.

At Union C, humiliation took the form of reputational distortion. Rumours circulated quietly but persistently. Performance concerns were implied but never documented. By the time the employee became aware of the narrative forming around him, it was already being treated as fact.

What made these moments particularly destabilising was not the humiliation itself, but the absence of proportion. None of the conduct described warranted public correction, escalation, or reputational damage. The response was not calibrated to the issue. It was calibrated to the audience.

In each case, the humiliation was performative rather than corrective. It was not designed to resolve a problem, but to establish a hierarchy. By stripping credibility publicly, the Dictator ensured that any future challenge from the same individual would arrive already weakened.

This tactic also served to neutralise witnesses. Once people saw how quickly standing out could result in exposure, discretion became self-defence. Silence was no longer passive. It was strategic.

In each case, the humiliation served the same purpose. It isolated the individual while instructing everyone else. The Dictator did not need to explain the rules. The room understood.

Demonstration Two: Moral Coercion

Moral coercion operates differently. It does not rely on spectacle, but on internal conflict.

At Union A, the employee was repeatedly placed in impossible positions. She was expected to uphold organisational values publicly while being asked to compromise them privately. When she hesitated, the pressure was reframed as concern.

Was she coping?

Was she committed?

Was she aligned with the organisation's goals?

None of these questions were neutral. Each implied that resistance was a personal failing rather than an ethical stance. Over time, the burden shifted. The problem was no longer the request, but her reluctance to comply.

At Union B, moral coercion arrived disguised as realism. The employee was told, explicitly and implicitly, that idealism had no place in the workplace. This is how things work, she was reminded. The implication was clear: values were optional, but consequences were not.

The choice presented was never fair. Uphold principles and risk isolation, or compromise quietly and remain safe. The Dictator did not need to issue threats. The structure did it for them.

At Union C, the coercion was transactional. Allegiance was rewarded with protection. Silence was framed as maturity. Speaking up was positioned as reckless, not just for the individual, but for others.

The unspoken message was devastatingly effective: your integrity has a cost, and others will pay it with you.

This is how moral coercion works.

It converts ethics into liability and turns self-betrayal into survival.

What distinguishes moral coercion from ordinary pressure is that it enlists the worker in their own containment. The individual is encouraged to internalise responsibility for the discomfort they are experiencing. The system remains unquestioned. The conscience becomes the battleground.

Over time, this produces exhaustion rather than rebellion.

Ethical tension is reframed as personal fragility.

The worker learns to pre-emptively soften objections, to downplay concerns, to second-guess instincts that once felt clear.

What looks from the outside like acquiescence is often the result of prolonged internal conflict.

The Dictator does not need to break people.

They only need them to doubt themselves.

Demonstration Three: Buying Allegiance

When fear and coercion are insufficient, loyalty is purchased.

At Union A, proximity to leadership became currency. Those who aligned themselves with the Dictator found doors opening. Opportunities appeared. Their mistakes were overlooked. Meanwhile, those who maintained distance noticed their influence diminish.

Nothing was stated explicitly.

No rules were written.

But patterns were clear.

At Union B, allegiance was rewarded through protection. Certain behaviours were tolerated for some and punished in others. The inconsistency was not accidental. It created a hierarchy of safety: those inside the circle and those outside it.

Workers learned quickly that fairness was not the metric. Alignment was.

At Union C, loyalty was bought through silence. Those who witnessed misconduct but said nothing were left untouched. Those who raised concerns found themselves suddenly exposed: scrutinised, questioned, and isolated. Over time, this created a second layer of enforcement: peers who had something to lose. Even those who disagreed with what was happening learned to keep their heads down. Self-preservation replaced solidarity.

The Dictator no longer needed to act directly. The system now protected itself.

Power Context: Why This Behaviour Is Protected

These dynamics persist because institutions often reward the very conditions that allow them to flourish.

High staff turnover is normalised as "the cost of doing business."

Core values are displayed but not enacted. Processes exist on paper but are selectively applied. Those who expose dysfunction are reframed as difficult, emotional, or incapable of coping with pressure. Attempts to seek accountability are frequently met with delay, deflection, or procedural fatigue. Complaints are siloed. Patterns are ignored. Individuals are treated as anomalies rather than signals.

In such environments, the Dictator is useful.

They contain dissent.

They keep complaints from travelling upward.

They maintain the appearance of order.

And so, they are protected.

The Psychological Effect on Others

The most corrosive impact of the Dictator is not what happens to the person targeted, but what happens to everyone else.

Witnesses learn to recalibrate. They stop asking questions. They avoid association. They lower their expectations of fairness. Over time, fear becomes background noise; ever-present, rarely named.

This recalibration is rarely conscious. Most witnesses do not experience themselves as choosing fear over integrity. Instead, they experience themselves as being sensible, realistic, or professional. Each small adjustment feels justified in isolation.

Over time, this creates a culture in which people do not merely comply, they anticipate. Behaviour is modified in advance of consequence. Questions go unasked. Concerns are self-edited. The absence of overt conflict is mistaken for stability, even as trust erodes quietly beneath the surface.

This is how authoritarian environments persist without constant enforcement. People learn the boundaries, and then police themselves.

People begin to believe that this is simply how workplaces function. That integrity is naïve. That speaking up is reckless. That survival requires accommodation.

This is how authoritarian control embeds itself quietly, without uniforms or slogans.

Recognition

If you recognise yourself in this chapter, you are not alone.

You may have been warned, explicitly or implicitly, that speaking up would affect others.

You may have been told to "be careful," to "think about the bigger picture," or to "not rock the boat."

You may have noticed that those who challenge the system disappear, while those who comply advance.

If loyalty is demanded but accountability is absent,

If integrity is reframed as betrayal,

If fear is normalised as professionalism, this is not conflict.

It is authoritarian control operating inside a workplace.

Looking Ahead

Recognition does not require immediate action. It requires clarity. Once the pattern is seen, it cannot be unseen. That recognition becomes the first quiet act of resistance, not loud, not performative, but stabilising.

The chapters that follow do not promise easy outcomes. They do not offer false reassurance or heroic myths. Instead, they provide understanding, strategy, and tools for navigating systems that were never designed to protect you. Because when power relies on silence, clarity is already a threat.

Recognising authoritarian control does not make a person calculating or cynical. It makes them oriented. Once the rules of the environment are revealed, continuing to act as though fairness will spontaneously emerge is not principled, it is unsafe.

Strategy, in this context, is not about deception or power-seeking. It is about understanding the terrain, conserving energy, and choosing responses that do not further expose you to harm.

When systems reward silence and punish integrity, discernment becomes essential.

The next chapter is not about abandoning values to survive, but about learning how to move within hostile structures without losing yourself in them. Because when the game is rigged, pretending it isn't does not make you ethical, it makes you vulnerable.

Playing The Game

THE NAYSAYER

The Naysayer plays for time. They turn every solution into a liability until progress collapses under its own weight.

RIGHT WITH YOU

There comes a point where doing the "right thing" no longer protects you. It exposes you.

This chapter is not an endorsement of cynicism.

It is an acknowledgement of reality.

When systems stop responding to good faith, strategy becomes survival.

Playing the game is not about winning favour or compromising values.

It is about staying intact long enough to make choices on your own terms.

Those who weaponise processes count on your reasonableness.

They rely on it.

They know that decent people hesitate, explain, give the benefit of the doubt, and assume shared standards still apply.

They don't.

This is the chapter where we say the quiet part out loud: once you are targeted, the rules change.

Not because you chose them to, but because someone else already did.

The Greater the Level, the Greater the Devil

Power does not become cleaner as it rises. It becomes more polished, until polish is no longer necessary.

When control is sufficiently entrenched, restraint often gives way to coercion, and aggression replaces subtlety.

At higher levels, harm is rarely crude. It is subtle, plausible, and procedural. Words are chosen carefully. Emails are vague by design. Meetings happen without minutes. Decisions are reframed as misunderstandings. Outcomes are described as inevitable rather than constructed.

And when that fails, the tactics escalate, not louder, but smarter.

The False Choice: Stay and Do Nothing

Workers are often presented with an unspoken ultimatum: endure quietly or risk everything. Staying feels safer. Doing nothing feels prudent. But this is the first trap.

1. The bully plays smarter, not harder.

Silence is not neutrality. It is information. When no resistance appears, tactics evolve. What began as exclusion becomes innuendo. What was informal becomes documented, selectively. The story is written without you, then handed back as fact.

2. You comply, and lose yourself.

Compliance has a cost. It erodes boundaries first, then identity. You begin to anticipate reactions, soften language, second-guess instincts.

Boundary breaches are rarely accidental. They are tests.

When no resistance follows, the breach becomes precedent.

When resistance does follow, it is reframed as defiance.

Stronger boundaries are not read as self-respect. They are interpreted as challenges.

Over time, the work becomes secondary to managing perception. You are still present, but no longer whole.

Compliance is not passivity. It is often the residue of repeated boundary testing.

This is how people disappear without ever leaving.

How the Choice Is Manufactured

The appearance of choice is itself a tactic.

Workers are rarely told directly to stay silent. Instead, conditions are created where speaking up feels irrational, disproportionate, or self-destructive. You are shown examples: others who "made things difficult" quietly vanished. You are reminded of what you stand to lose. You are told, sometimes gently, sometimes not, that this is not the hill to die on.

The brilliance of this mechanism is that compliance feels self-directed. No explicit threat is required. Fear does the work instead.

Over time, the question stops being:

Is this right?

And becomes:

Is this worth it?

That shift marks the moment the game is fully in play.

When "Reasonable" Becomes a Trap

During COVID, a seemingly mundane issue was raised: access to bathrooms.

Visitors were required to obtain a pass to use bathrooms on both levels of the building. These passes had to be returned and sanitised at reception. Later, an option was introduced to extend one bathroom on a single floor for broader use. That bathroom was designated for men only.

Concerns were raised quietly. Not about inconvenience, but about safety and equity. It was acknowledged openly that the space had been used by drug users, that syringes were common, brushed off with the explanation that "this is what happens in Sydney."

What mattered most was not the policy itself, but the process attached to dissent.

Those with concerns were asked not to raise them collectively, but to approach leadership directly, one-on-one. On its face, this appeared reasonable, even respectful. A direct line. An open door. A chance to be heard.

In practice, it served a different function.

By funnelling objections into private channels, dissent was atomised. There was no shared context, no collective comparison, no way to test whether concerns were isolated or widespread. What looked like responsiveness became a sorting mechanism: a way to identify who was willing to contest authority, and who would stay silent.

In practice, it functioned like a sporting exercise: dissent was provoked, observed, and scored. Those in control learned who would push back, who would hesitate, who would comply, and adjusted their tactics accordingly.

This is a familiar tactic in environments where control matters more than resolution. The issue becomes the bait. The response becomes the data. Those who speak up are quietly marked as potential defectors, a dictator's worst nightmare, not because they are unreasonable, but because they are visible.

The bathrooms were never the point.

The point was to make resistance costly, personal, and exposed, while maintaining the appearance of reasonableness throughout.

When Reasonableness Is Used Against You

Reasonableness assumes reciprocity. It presumes shared norms and good faith. In abusive systems, these assumptions become liabilities.

A reasonable person explains.

An unreasonable system records selectively.

A reasonable person waits.

An unreasonable system moves ahead without them.

A reasonable person trusts the process.

An unreasonable system exploits it.

Recognising this is not paranoia. It is pattern recognition.

The Myth of the Reasonable Actor

Workplace systems love the idea of the reasonable person because it places the burden of equilibrium on the individual. If you remain calm, professional, and cooperative, the assumption is that the system will respond in kind. But abusive systems are not built around reason.

They are built around control. Reasonableness becomes a trap because it delays recognition. It encourages over-explanation. It rewards patience in environments where patience is interpreted as permission.

A reasonable response to an unreasonable environment does not restore balance. It reinforces the imbalance.

What often follows is a fishing expedition. The reasonable person is encouraged to explain, clarify, and "tell me more." Information is gathered not to understand, but to confirm a pre-made decision.

Details are later extracted, reframed, or selectively quoted, leaving the individual disoriented, unsure which part of their account caused harm, or how to proceed without causing more.

Reasonableness becomes a liability because it supplies the system with raw material, while the outcome has already been decided.

Understanding this is not about becoming reactive or aggressive.

It is about releasing the expectation that fairness will emerge organically, if you just behave well enough.

Demonstrations in Practice

In Union A, concern was framed as care. Conversations were framed as check-ins. But every disclosure was quietly retained. Personal context became professional leverage. When pressure mounted, the worker's openness was reframed as instability, and their commitment reinterpreted as unreliability. Nothing overt occurred. That was the point. The record spoke louder than the reality.

In Union B, the shift was social before it was procedural. Invitations stopped. Information arrived late. Small absences were noticed, then noted. When the worker attempted to clarify what had changed, they were told nothing had. Their response: confusion, was later described as defensiveness. The narrative hardened before any formal process began.

In Union C, the tactic was a contradiction. Instructions were given verbally, then denied. Decisions were attributed to consensus that never occurred. When challenged, the worker was accused of misremembering. Each instance was minor in isolation. Together, they created a fog in which certainty became impossible, and doubt became self-directed.

Different environments. Same playbook.

What These Stories Have in Common

In each case, the harm was not delivered through a single decisive act. It emerged through accumulation. Minor distortions. Small omissions. Plausible deniability stacked carefully on top of itself.

None of these workers were accused outright. None were confronted directly.

Each was slowly repositioned, from trusted contributor to potential liability. By the time formal processes appeared, the outcome already felt justified.

This is how systems avoid accountability. They do not need to prove wrongdoing if they can manufacture doubt. And doubt, once internalised, does most of the damage for them.

Isolation as a Method

Isolation is not always exclusion. Sometimes it is surveillance disguised as concern. Sometimes confidentiality is weaponised as silence. Sometimes it is the slow narrowing of who feels safe to talk to.

The goal is simple: break the feedback loop.

If you cannot compare notes, you cannot see the pattern.

If you doubt your perception, you will not trust your conclusions.

Playing the game means understanding this dynamic early, and countering it deliberately.

Why Isolation Works So Well

Isolation is effective because it disrupts regulation.

Humans orient through others. We test reality socially. When that feedback is removed or made unsafe, uncertainty multiplies.

The body responds before the mind does. Vigilance increases. Sleep fragments. Thinking narrows. The worker becomes easier to manage, not because they are weaker, but because they are alone.

This physiological dimension is rarely acknowledged, yet it explains why people stay longer than they intended and doubt themselves more than the evidence warrants. Isolation does not just silence dissent, it exhausts it.

Nothing Is Off-Limits

Once a person is marked for removal, boundaries dissolve.

Private relationships become professional currency. Associations are scrutinised. Innocent interactions are recast as impropriety.

Innuendo is deployed because it contaminates without requiring proof. Sexuality, friendships, and perceived loyalties become tools.

We have seen how quickly suggestion replaces evidence. How easily credibility is undermined by implication alone. Once seeded, these narratives are hard to dislodge, not because they are true, but because they are uncomfortable to challenge.

This is not accidental. It is strategic.

The Catch-Cry

Every system has one. A phrase that sounds reasonable while excusing unreasonable conduct.

"It's none of your business."

"This is just how it works."

"You're overthinking it."

These are not explanations. They are containment tools.

Releasing the Guilt

Many readers will struggle here.

They will worry that strategy makes them complicit. That adapting means conceding. That playing the game turns them into something they are not.

It doesn't.

Why This Feels Uncomfortable

Playing the game feels uncomfortable because it violates the story many people hold about themselves. They believe integrity should be enough. That transparency should protect them. That systems designed to promote justice will, at minimum, recognise it.

When those beliefs collide with reality, the discomfort is often turned inward. People question their own values rather than the environment that exploits them.

This chapter asks for a different reframe: integrity is not proven by how much harm you absorb. It is preserved by knowing when to stop offering yourself to a system that has already shown you how it will respond.

Strategy is not manipulation.

Boundaries are not betrayal.

Silence is not consent.

You are not required to offer your integrity up for sacrifice simply because someone else has decided to misuse it. Refusing to be naïve in a hostile environment is not moral failure, it is self-preservation.

Win. Lose. Draw.

From the outside, outcomes are often judged harshly. Inside the system, they are rarely neutral.

- Winning does not mean vindication. It often means survival with cost.
- Losing does not mean you were wrong. It often means the system closed ranks.
- Drawing is not stagnation. It is often the only way to exit intact.

These outcomes are not measures of worth. They are products of power, timing, and tolerance for exposure.

Why Outcomes Are Not Verdicts

Readers often want to know how to ensure a win. That question makes sense, but it rests on a false premise. Outcomes in these environments are not adjudications of truth. They are reflections of leverage.

Winning can mean exposure with scars.

Losing can mean silence with consequences.

Drawing can mean leaving before the final move is played.

None of these outcomes determine whether you were right. They only determine what the system was willing to tolerate.

What they do reflect is something else entirely.

Outcomes often reveal the individual's tolerance for risk, exposure, and loss. Not their integrity, intelligence, or credibility. They show how much a person was willing, or able, to endure in pursuit of truth, safety, or principle at a particular moment in time.

Choosing silence can be an act of protection. Leaving can be an act of clarity. Staying and fighting can be an act of conviction, or a cost too high to sustain. None of these choices are moral failures. They are adaptive responses to constrained power.

The mistake is not the choice itself, but allowing the outcome to be retroactively rewritten as a judgement of character.

Understanding this distinction matters.

It prevents people from measuring their worth by results that were never fully within their control.

Playing the Game Without Losing Yourself

Strategy does not require abandoning values. It requires calibration.

It means documenting without narrating.

Responding without over-explaining.

Choosing silence where explanations will be distorted.

Preserving evidence while conserving energy.

It means knowing when engagement feeds the narrative, and when restraint protects you.

This is not cowardice. It is discernment.

This chapter is not about victory. It is about positioning. About staying upright in a tilted field.

Because what comes next is a consequence.

In the chapters that follow, we examine what happens when the game is won, when it is lost, and when it is drawn.

We look at duty, documentation, and the cost of staying longer than is safe.

For now, remember this:

Playing the game does not mean accepting the rules.

It means surviving them, long enough to choose your exit, your stance, and your truth.

Knowledge Is Power

THE HOOLIGAN

Knowledge threatens the Hooligan.
So they shout it down,
break the conversation,
and make thinking unsafe.

RIGHT WITH YOU

There is a belief many workers carry quietly with them into employment: that knowledge is protection.

Know your rights. Read the policy. Understand the law.

If something goes wrong, you will be able to name it, challenge it, and be shielded from harm.

This belief is rarely interrogated because it feels reasonable.

It is taught implicitly through induction programs, compliance training, and public campaigns.

It is reinforced through posters on lunchroom walls and slogans embedded in organisational culture.

The implication is simple: informed workers are safer workers.

But this belief does not hold up under scrutiny.

If it did, the most protected people in workplaces would be those trained in employment law, policy, and process. Union officials. Workplace advocates. Delegates. Human resources professionals. People whose working lives are shaped by legislation, rights, and procedural fairness.

And yet, as this book demonstrates, those are often the very people who are targeted, isolated, and pushed out.

This chapter exists to explain that paradox.

Knowledge is not meaningless. But it is also not the protection it is sold to be. Understanding why requires separating two ideas that are often collapsed into one: knowledge and power.

The Promise of Knowledge

Workers are taught that the employment relationship is governed by rules. That there are laws, standards, and obligations that apply equally to all parties. That if those rules are breached, remedies exist. That the system, while imperfect, is fundamentally fair.

This framing encourages workers to invest in understanding their rights. To read enterprise agreements. To attend training. To learn the language of policy and procedure. To believe that knowledge equips them to navigate risk.

There is value in this. Knowledge allows people to recognise when something is wrong. It provides language for discomfort. It creates reference points beyond personal feeling. It is often the first step in realising that harm is not imagined.

But knowledge also creates expectations. It leads people to believe that once a breach is identified, the system will respond proportionately. That naming the issue will lead to correction. That the presence of rules implies enforcement.

This is where the promise quietly fractures.

The Paradox of the Informed Worker

One of the least acknowledged realities of dysfunctional workplaces is that informed workers are often perceived as a threat rather than an asset.

Knowledge disrupts asymmetry. It limits plausible deniability. It introduces the possibility of scrutiny. Even when it is never explicitly deployed, its presence alters the power dynamic.

An informed worker does not need to be confrontational to unsettle a system. They simply need to be able to recognise inconsistency. To remember what was said. To understand what should have happened and what did not.

This awareness alone can be destabilising in environments that rely on informality, selective enforcement, or narrative control.

As a result, knowledge can become a liability.

Not because it is wrong, but because it cannot be easily neutralised without effort. And effort, in these environments, is often expended not on correction, but on containment.

This is why retaliation rarely announces itself as retaliation. It is more likely to appear as a process. As a concern. As performance management. As wellbeing intervention. The language shifts, but the objective remains the same: to reassert control without acknowledging conflict.

For the informed worker, this can be particularly disorienting. They recognise the misalignment between what is happening and what should be happening. But recognition does not equate to protection. In fact, it can intensify vulnerability.

Knowledge Without Power

To understand why knowledge alone does not protect workers, it is necessary to understand how power operates in employment relationships.

Power determines not only what rules exist, but how they are interpreted, when they are enforced, and against whom.

It shapes which breaches are visible and which are ignored. Which voices are heard and which are reframed.

In most workplaces, power does not sit evenly. Employers control resources, information flow, process initiation, and outcome framing. They decide when something becomes "formal." They determine what is documented, what is escalated, and what is resolved quietly.

In this context, knowledge does not function as armour. It functions as context. It allows a worker to see what is happening, but it does not guarantee that what is seen will be addressed.

This distinction matters. When workers believe knowledge should protect them, its failure feels personal. They assume they misapplied it. That they did not speak up correctly. That they chose the wrong moment or the wrong words.

The problem is not misuse. The problem is misplaced expectations.

The Misplaced Burden

One of the most effective ways responsibility is shifted away from systems is by placing the burden of protection onto individuals.

Workers are encouraged to be proactive. To raise concerns early. To engage constructively. To manage relationships. To build resilience. To access support. To document. To reflect. To self-regulate.

None of these actions are inherently unreasonable. But when they replace organisational responsibility, they become mechanisms of deflection.

The implicit message becomes: if harm continues, you have not done enough.

Not enough communication.

Not enough documentation.

Not enough self-care.

Not enough adaptability.

This inversion is subtle, and it is powerful. It transforms systemic failure into individual inadequacy. It keeps attention focused downward, even when the source of harm sits higher up the hierarchy.

For informed workers, this burden is heavier. They are expected not only to comply, but to model best practice. To tolerate inconsistency while explaining it. To absorb contradiction without reacting. Their knowledge becomes something to manage rather than something that protects them.

Over time, this dynamic erodes clarity. The worker begins to question their own interpretation. To wonder whether they are being unreasonable. To second-guess instincts that are, in fact, accurate. This is not confusion born of ignorance. It is confusion produced by exposure to a system that rewards silence and reframes dissent.

Reframing Knowledge

Understanding the limits of knowledge is not an argument against it. It is an argument for using it differently. Knowledge is not armour. It does not stop harm from occurring. It does not compel systems to behave ethically. It does not enforce itself. What knowledge does provide is orientation.

It allows workers to recognise patterns rather than internalise them. To identify breaches rather than personalise outcomes. To distinguish between isolated incidents and systemic behaviour. To understand that what feels chaotic often follows a recognisable logic. This shift is subtle but significant. When knowledge is reframed as context rather than protection, it relieves workers of a false responsibility. They are no longer tasked with making the system fair through understanding alone. They are able to see where responsibility actually sits. This reframing also creates a necessary pause. It interrupts the urge to act prematurely, to explain, to fix, to over-disclose. It allows knowledge to be held rather than immediately deployed. That restraint is not weakness. It is discernment.

From Knowledge to Accountability

Once knowledge is understood as orientation, a different question emerges.

Not "What should I do?" but "Who was required to act?"

This question shifts attention away from worker behaviour and toward organisational obligation. It prepares the ground for accountability by clarifying where duty lies.

It also explains why knowledge alone feels insufficient. Because it is not meant to carry the weight of enforcement. That burden belongs elsewhere.

This is the point at which many workers experience a moment of clarity that can be unsettling. They realise that the system did not fail because it was unaware. It failed because it did not act.

That recognition is not cynical. It is stabilising. It replaces confusion with proportion. It restores a sense of reality that prolonged exposure to contradiction often erodes.

What This Chapter Asks of the Reader

This chapter does not ask you to confront, escalate, or resolve. It asks you to see clearly.

To recognise that knowledge did not fail you.

That understanding of your rights was not naïve.

That harm persisting in the presence of knowledge is not evidence of personal inadequacy.

It asks you to let go of the belief that protection was ever meant to rest solely with you.

What comes next is not strategy or instruction.

It is a clarification of responsibility.

Because when knowledge meets obligation, the conversation changes. The question is no longer whether you understood the rules, but whether those entrusted with power honoured them.

That is where accountability begins.

And it is where this book now turns.

The problem was never a lack of knowledge.

They know employment law.

They rely on it.

They invoke it when it suits them.

And they break it, deliberately, against their own employees, while publicly campaigning for the rights of workers.

The Employer's Duty

THE MARTYR

The Martyr speaks of responsibility while avoiding it. They carry the narrative of sacrifice so no one asks what was done.

RIGHT WITH YOU

Australian workers have rights, and employers have obligations.

This is not an aspirational language.

It is the legal baseline, or, at least, it's supposed to be.

Among the most fundamental of these obligations is an employer's duty of care under work health and safety legislation. Historically, that duty was interpreted narrowly; focused on slips, trips, physical injuries, and visible hazards. Psychological harm was acknowledged, but often treated as secondary, subjective, or unfortunate collateral.

That framing has now collapsed.

That collapse has not occurred in isolation.

Alongside the recognition of psychosocial hazards and the Positive Duty, sexual harassment has been brought squarely within work health and safety enforcement, at both federal and state levels. Domestic and family violence is now recognised as a workplace issue, not only through leave entitlements, but through expanded support pathways, including Legal Aid and 1800 RESPECT.

These developments reflect the same legal truth: harm does not need to be physical, public, or sudden to trigger duty. It need only be foreseeable, unmanaged, and permitted to persist.

The introduction of the *Work Health and Safety (Managing Psychosocial Hazards at Work) Code of Practice 2024*, alongside the *Positive Duty* provisions, marks a formal recognition of what workers have long known:

Harm at work is not limited to the physical, and it is rarely accidental.

Psychological injury does not arise from individual fragility. It arises from environments. From systems. From decisions made, and not made, by those with power.

Importantly, these developments do not create new moral obligations. They clarify existing ones. The law has not become stricter. It has become more honest. It now names, explicitly, what was previously minimised or ignored: delay, inaction, reputational harm, procedural abuse, complaint suppression and the mishandling of sexual harassment or violence-related disclosures are not neutral administrative choices. They are workplace hazards.

This chapter sits here for a reason. After knowledge comes responsibility. After awareness comes duty.

The goal is not to drop down, but to rise up,
and become an employer of choice.

~~~~~~~~
~~~~~~~~

Knowing the Law vs Following the Law

Large employers are rarely ignorant of employment law.

They are saturated with it.

Internal counsel, external legal advisors, employer associations, policy frameworks, flowcharts, and training modules exist precisely to ensure legal awareness. Knowledge is embedded, distributed, and continuously reinforced.

The problem, then, is not a lack of understanding. It is the selective application of that understanding.

Legal advice operates at multiple levels. At the narrow end, it provides tactical guidance on individual matters. At the broader end, employer associations shape norms: what can be delayed, reframed, absorbed, or defended. One is specific. The other is systemic. Together, they create a buffer between obligation and consequence.

In this environment, compliance becomes conditional rather than principled. Law is followed when it aligns with organisational interest and managed when it does not. What appears, from the outside, as inconsistency or failure is often the product of coordinated interpretation rather than oversight.

This is why knowledge alone does not protect workers. It was never absent on the other side of the table.

This distinction between knowing the law and following it becomes clearest not in dramatic breaches, but in what is allowed to stretch on.

The introduction of psychosocial hazard obligations and the Positive Duty exposes this gap. Employers are no longer permitted to wait for damage to crystallise before responding. They are required to anticipate risk, identify hazards, and act early.

Much of the harm described in this book did not occur in moments of overt aggression, but in long stretches of silence.

In delays.

In "we're looking into it."

In procedural limbo.

What was once defended as caution is now recognised for what it often is: avoidance.

A Little Bit of a Delay

Delay is one of the most effective tools available to an employer who does not wish to act.

It appears benign. Reasonable, even. Time is needed to investigate. To consult. To consider all perspectives. But delay has consequences, and those consequences are rarely borne by the organisation. They are borne by the worker.

Under the psychosocial hazards framework, prolonged uncertainty is no longer a neutral state. It is a risk factor. The longer a complaint remains unresolved, the greater the likelihood of psychological harm: anxiety, hypervigilance, reputational damage, and deterioration of health.

Delay does not merely enable harm. It becomes a hazard in its own right.

At a macro level, this avoidance often hides behind:

- policies that exist on paper but not in practice
- complaint mechanisms that are technically available but functionally inaccessible
- archaic systems for leave, flexibility, and support, including leave that is formally approved, then later withdrawn or rendered unusable due to "low staffing levels" or "operational / business needs"
- the quiet presence of gatekeepers

In practice, these mechanisms give the appearance of accommodation while ensuring the underlying conditions remain unchanged.

Gatekeepers sit at the micro level. They control what moves upward and what stalls. What is framed as serious and what is dismissed as interpersonal. What reaches decision-makers and what quietly expires.

The Positive Duty dismantles the protection this role once offered. Employers can no longer rely on the absence of a complaint as evidence of safety. Silence is not compliance. Silence is often the product of fear.

Which raises a confronting question; one that workers ask long before regulators do:

Do some organisations tolerate bully managers,
because fear keeps complaints from moving?
Because if nothing reaches the top,
nothing needs to be addressed?

The law now answers these questions indirectly. Whatever the motive, the outcome is no longer defensible.

When People Do Not Believe You

One of the most destabilising experiences for workers is not the initial harm, but the disbelief that follows it.

False allegations, reputational smearing, and quiet narrative shifts are effective precisely because they exploit a cultural assumption: that institutions are neutral and individuals are emotional. That systems are rational and complainants are reactive.

Under these conditions, it becomes easier to discredit a worker than to confront organisational failure.

The result is predictable.

Complaints are minimised. Credibility is questioned.

The worker is reframed as difficult, unstable, or conspiratorial.

Over time, this disbelief is internalised.

Workers begin to question their own perceptions:

Did it really happen?

Was it that bad?

Am I being oversensitive?

Each "maybe" erodes certainty, not because the harm was unclear, but because it has been systematically reframed. This is not introspection. It is induced doubt. And it is one of the most effective ways institutions neutralise resistance without ever having to deny the facts outright.

This response is not accidental. It is structural.

Psychosocial safety obligations now recognise that reputational harm and disbelief are not secondary issues. They are central to how harm is compounded. Being disbelieved is not merely hurtful. It isolates, escalates distress, and discourages further reporting.

The law no longer permits employers to outsource disbelief to process. Investigations that drag on, fragment evidence, or quietly resolve without accountability do not neutralise harm. They amplify it.

Union A

In Union A, the employer's duty was triggered early.

Concerns were raised. Indicators of harm were present. The risk was neither abstract nor speculative. It was known.

What followed, however, was not a proportionate response to that risk. Instead of containment, there was drift. Instead of early intervention, there was procedural hesitation. Responsibility moved laterally rather than upward, and urgency dissolved into process.

From a psychosocial safety perspective, this period matters more than the originating incident. Once an employer is on notice, the obligation shifts. The question is no longer whether harm might occur, but how it will be prevented. In Union A, prevention never materialised.

The worker remained exposed: to uncertainty, to reputational speculation, to an environment that continued unchanged while the issue sat unresolved. Meetings were postponed. Decisions were deferred. Communication was sparse and carefully non-committal. What was framed as caution functioned, in effect, as containment of the complaint rather than the hazard.

Under the 2024 psychosocial framework, this type of response is no longer defensible. Prolonged ambiguity is a recognised contributor to psychological injury. The employer's failure here was not an overt act of retaliation, but a sustained absence of protection.

The environment itself became the source of harm.

The duty was not breached in a moment. It was breached over a lengthy period of time.

Union B

Union B illustrates a different, but equally common, failure of employer duty: the decision to allow exposure to continue while issues are "being looked into."

The worker had already been identified as vulnerable by virtue of having raised concerns.

That alone should have triggered heightened care.

Instead, they were left to navigate the same environment, with the same actors, and the same informal power dynamics. Complicated by the knowledge that they had spoken up. This is where psychosocial risk compounds.

The absence of visible action sends a clear message to others in the workplace: nothing has changed. Gossip fills the vacuum. Speculation replaces information. The worker's credibility is quietly tested, not through evidence, but through repetition.

From a Positive Duty standpoint, this represents a critical failure. Employers are required to act before harm escalates, not after it becomes undeniable. Allowing a worker to remain in an environment where reputational damage and informal retaliation are foreseeable is not neutrality. It is exposure.

What is particularly notable in Union B is that the harm was not driven by a single decision, but by accumulation. Each day without clarity, each interaction left unmanaged, each silence from leadership reinforced the same message: the worker was on their own.

Psychosocial safety is not maintained through reassurance. It is maintained through action. In Union B, action never arrived.

Union C

Union C demonstrates the most procedurally sophisticated failure, where systems designed to ensure fairness were used in ways that actively undermined it.

Here, the employer's response relied heavily on documentation, investigation, and formal process.

On the surface, this appeared compliant.

In reality, it obscured the underlying hazard and shifted focus away from prevention.

The worker, meanwhile, was required to respond, clarify, and correct, repeatedly, while the environment that caused the harm remained intact.

Under contemporary psychosocial standards, this approach is deeply problematic. Process does not discharge duty if it does not reduce risk. Investigations that run parallel to ongoing exposure do not neutralise harm. They often intensify it by prolonging uncertainty and reinforcing power imbalance.

The Positive Duty makes this explicit. Employers cannot satisfy their obligations by appearing active while leaving hazards in place. Where harm is foreseeable, containment and prevention must occur alongside any formal review. In Union C, the employer chose order over care, and record-keeping over protection.

The result was predictable: psychological harm deepened, trust eroded, and the system that claimed neutrality became an active contributor to the injury it was meant to address.

Why These Sections Matter

Taken together, Unions A, B, and C do not represent anomalies. They represent variations of the same failure:

A refusal, explicit or implicit, to treat psychological safety with the same seriousness as physical risk.

The law has now named this failure.

What remains is accountability.

The Pattern the Law Now Recognises

Viewed side by side, Unions A, B, and C differ in culture, structure, and method, but not in outcome.

In each case, the employer was on notice.

In each case, psychosocial risk was identifiable, foreseeable, and escalating.

And in each case, the response prioritised organisational control, exercised by those in power through institutional systems, over worker protection.

Delay replaced intervention.

Process substituted for prevention.

Silence was treated as neutrality.

Under the Positive Duty framework, these are not grey areas or unfortunate misjudgements; they are failures of obligation.

The law now recognises that harm does not require intent, escalation, or a dramatic incident to be real.

It requires only an employer who knows, or ought reasonably to know, that a risk exists and chooses not to act.

What these three unions demonstrate is not a lack of awareness, but a shared tolerance for exposure to foreseeable psychological harm, through delay, silence, and unmanaged power imbalance.

Different tactics, same breach.

The pattern was always visible.

The law has simply stopped looking away.

What the Law Now Makes Clear

The developments in psychosocial safety and Positive Duty do not rewrite the past.

They expose it.

They make explicit what workers have lived through quietly for years:

- that delay is not neutral
- that silence is not safety
- that inaction is a choice
- and that harm does not need to be dramatic to be real

Employers are no longer permitted to wait until damage is undeniable.

They are required to act when risk is visible.

And risk has always been visible.

What Positive Duty Actually Means

Positive Duty changes the question employers are required to ask.

Traditionally, workplace obligations were framed reactively.

An employer responded after a complaint was made, after harm was established, or after a threshold was crossed.

The burden, in practice, often fell on the worker to identify the problem, endure it long enough to evidence it, and then withstand the consequences of raising it.

Positive Duty reverses that logic.

Under a Positive Duty framework, employers are required to actively prevent harm, not merely respond to it.

This includes taking reasonable and proportionate steps to identify psychosocial hazards, assess the risks they pose, and eliminate or minimise those risks before injury occurs.

Waiting for a formal complaint is no longer a defence.

In practical terms, this means:

- Employers cannot rely on silence as evidence of safety.
- Known risks must be addressed even if no one has lodged a complaint.
- Delay, inaction, and procedural stalling can themselves constitute exposure to harm.
- Systems, behaviours, and power dynamics must be examined, including differences in agency and control created by uniforms, rosters, duties, reporting lines, scheduling authority, and decision-making power. Not just individual conduct.

Power imbalance is not abstract; it is embedded in how work is allocated, controlled, and enforced.

Positive Duty recognises that harm at work is often predictable, cumulative, and environmental. Psychological injury does not require a single dramatic incident. It can arise from prolonged uncertainty, unmanaged conflict, reputational damage, isolation, or the sustained failure to act. Importantly, Positive Duty is not about perfection. It does not require employers to eliminate all risk or foresee every outcome. It requires good faith, early intervention, and reasonable action when risk is visible. What it removes is plausible deniability. Employers are no longer assessed solely on how they respond once damage is undeniable, but on what they did, or failed to do, when warning signs were already present.

In other words, the question is no longer: Did we act once someone broke?

It is now: What did we do to prevent them from breaking in the first place?

In Closing

This chapter is not about bad employers. It is about breached obligations.

It is about organisations that know the law, understand the standards, and promote the language of safety, while failing to extend it inward.

It is the fact they all know employment law,
but break it
against their own employees
while running campaigns that promote
workers' rights.

That contradiction is no longer philosophical.

It is legal.

And the law has finally stopped pretending otherwise.

The Pen is Mightier than the Sword

THE WARRIOR

The Warrior knows the pen outlasts the threat. They document until power can no longer pretend.

RIGHT WITH YOU

Documentation is not neutral.

It is not busywork.

And it is not optional.

In environments where power is misused, documentation becomes the line between reality and narrative. It is how truth survives distortion. It is how memory is stabilised when gaslighting attempts to rewrite events. And it is often the only thing standing between a worker and erasure.

The process is demanding. You spend your working hours navigating harm, and your personal hours recording it.

That double load is exhausting.

But without a record, harm remains anecdotal, and anecdotes are easily dismissed.

This chapter is not about writing beautifully.

It is about writing accurately, consistently, and strategically.

Why Documentation Matters

In theory, workplaces are meant to operate on evidence.

In practice, they operate on credibility.

And credibility is shaped long before any formal process begins.

When something goes wrong, the first question is rarely *what happened?*

It is *who do we believe?*

Documentation answers that question quietly, before it is asked.

A contemporaneous record:

- anchors events in time
- reduces reliance on memory under stress
- creates patterns where single incidents can be dismissed
- protects you from later narrative shifts

Without documentation, the system defaults to hierarchy.

With it, the system has something to contend with.

The Worker Diary: Your First Line of Defence

Your worker diary is not a journal.

It is not a place to vent.

It is a log of facts.

Think of it as a ledger.

Each entry should include:

- **Date**
- **Time**
- **Location or medium** (in person, phone, email, meeting)
- **Who was present**
- **What was said or done** (verbatim where possible)
- **Immediate impact** (on work, safety, wellbeing)
- **Any witnesses or documents**

Keep language neutral. Describe behaviour, not character.

Observable Behaviour Includes Non-Verbal Conduct

Neutral documentation does not stop at words.

It also includes observable, physical behaviours, such as:

- hand gestures
- body positioning or proximity
- facial expressions
- posture
- tone, volume, and intonation

For example, instead of writing "they were intimidating", a neutral record might note:

"They raised their voice, stood within arm's length, pointed repeatedly, and spoke over me."

Or:

"The comment was delivered with a raised voice and sarcastic tone, accompanied by dismissive hand gestures."

These are not interpretations.

They are descriptions of conduct.

Why This Matters

Tone and body language are often where power is exercised, and where harm occurs, while remaining deniable.

By documenting what was seen and heard, rather than how it felt, workers:

- preserve accuracy,
- avoid subjective framing, and
- capture behaviours that often explain why words alone caused harm

Over time, patterns of non-verbal conduct can be as revealing as spoken statements.

A Quiet Reminder

You are not documenting emotions.

You are documenting what happened in the room.

Neutral records that include observable non-verbal behaviour travel further, and last longer, than conclusions ever will.

Instead of *"they were intimidating"*, write *"they raised their voice, stood close, and said..."*

This discipline matters.

Neutral records travel further.

Why Written Responses Matter

When matters may later become disciplinary, a further discipline applies:

Ask for responses in writing. This is not adversarial. It is clarifying.

Requesting a written response:

- fixes the issue in time,
- requires the employer to commit to a position, and
- prevents later reconstruction of intent

If an employer chooses not to respond, or is unable to, that silence itself becomes informative.

Over time, it allows a worker to demonstrate that:

- concerns were raised,
- opportunities to respond were provided, and
- the matter was not treated as serious by the employer at the time

Silence, in this context, is not neutral.

It is part of the record.

How Silence Functions as Evidence

In contested processes, employers often argue seriousness retrospectively.

Contemporaneous records answer that argument quietly.

If an issue was raised in writing and no response followed, it becomes difficult to later claim urgency, gravity, or immediacy, without explaining the absence.

This is not about trapping anyone.

It is about preserving proportion.

The Principle

Neutral documentation does not demand agreement. It invites a response. And when no response comes, the record speaks for itself. Your diary is not written for today. It is written for six months from now, when fatigue has set in and details blur.

Identifying Mid and Long-Term Impact

Documentation is not only about capturing what happens in the moment. It is also about tracing what unfolds over time.

Many forms of workplace harm do not present as single, decisive incidents. They emerge gradually, through movement, reshuffling, and justification layered over justification.

By the time the impact becomes visible, the original "reasons" are often forgotten, or reframed as operational necessity. This is why documenting impact across time matters as much as documenting events.

What Mid and Long-Term Impact Can Look Like

Over weeks or months, patterns often emerge that are invisible in isolation:

- repeated changes in work location, role, or reporting lines
- shifting "reasons" for decisions that do not withstand comparison
- progressive isolation from familiar teams or supports
- loss of continuity in work, supervision, or legal advice
- erosion of confidence, stability, or professional standing

Each change may be justified on paper.

Together, they tell a different story.

From Incident to Pattern

One employee described being moved from site to site, each time for a stated "reason."

Only when she stepped back and reviewed her records did the pattern become clear: the reasons did not align, repeat, or hold.

What emerged instead was a strategy of destabilisation.

Once she recognised the pattern, she adjusted, not emotionally, but structurally.

Measures were put in place to prevent further movement without explanation.

When relocation was no longer possible, the pressure shifted elsewhere: teams were restructured, then management layers, then legal support.

This is how systemic harm adapts when resisted.

What to Record When Looking Longitudinally

In addition to daily entries, it can be useful to maintain a separate impact log that tracks:

- cumulative changes to role, location, or conditions
- frequency and timing of "reasons" given
- points where justification changes or contradicts earlier explanations
- downstream effects on wellbeing, capacity, or performance
- organisational responses once resistance or boundaries appear

This is not about interpretation.

It is about sequence.

Why This Matters

Institutions often defend harm by pointing to any one decision and asking, "What's wrong with that?"

Documentation over time answers a different question:

What is the effect of all of this, taken together?

Mid- and long-term records reveal:

- intent without speculation
- strategy without accusation
- impact without exaggeration

They show that harm does not require a single dramatic act.

It only requires persistence, authority, and plausible explanations.

A Quiet Truth

By the time people start asking whether something feels destabilising, the documentation often already shows that it is.

Not because the worker imagined it, but because the pattern has been building all along.

What to Document (And What People Forget To)

Most people document the "big" events.

They forget the small ones.

That is a mistake.

You should document:

- inappropriate comments (even when framed as jokes)
  * When a concern is raised and the response is "It was just a joke," this is not clarification. It is deflection.

Document:

- the original comment
- who was present
- the response when concern was raised, and
- change in tone, behaviour, or treatment afterwards

A defensive reframe is often the first indicator that the comment was not benign.

- changes in tone after you raise a concern
- shifting expectations or contradictory instructions
- exclusions from meetings or information
- sudden scrutiny of your work
- delays, deflections, or silence after complaints
- informal conversations that later become conversations, verbal directions, or casual remarks that later reappear as "official positions"

Patterns are built from repetition, not drama.

Adding Accountability to Phone Calls

One of the most common tactics in contested processes is the *phantom phone call*.

"We tried to reach you" claims of attempted contact without date, time, method, or sender.

When this is asserted, request clarification in writing:

- the date and time of the attempt
- who made the call
- their role
- the purpose of the contact

Vague claims of outreach are not evidence.

Specifics are.

"We left a message" claims that a message was left, without confirmation of content, timing, or receipt.

If a matter was serious, the contents of the message, and the method used, should be identifiable.

Silence, ambiguity, or refusal to clarify is itself part of the record.

"You didn't respond" allegations of non-response without acknowledging timing, context, or opportunity to reply

If the issue was deemed urgent or disciplinary, a reasonable opportunity to respond would ordinarily be provided.

Where no such opportunity existed, this may indicate the process is being used to pressure or intimidate, rather than to seek response.

If it isn't documented, it didn't happen.

After every phone call, create a follow-up email.

Even if it feels awkward.

Example: *Subject: Follow-up to our phone call today*

Hi [Name],

Further to our phone conversation at approximately 10:15am today, my understanding is that:

– [brief point one]

– [brief point two]

Please let me know if I have misunderstood anything.

Regards, [Your name]

This does three things:

1. **It creates a timestamp**
2. **It locks the narrative**
3. **It shifts the burden of correction onto them**

Silence becomes informative.

Example Evidence Collection Tool 1:

Date	Time	Event	People Present	Evidence	Notes

Use a simple table or document with consistent headings and attach:

- emails
- calendar invites
- screenshots
- meeting agendas
- file versions showing edits or deletions

Do not over-explain. Let the material speak.

Example Evidence Collection Tool 2:

The Pattern Timeline

Once you have multiple entries, step back.

Lay events out chronologically and ask:

- What changed after I raised concerns?
- When did scrutiny begin?
- Who became involved, and when?
- What behaviours repeat?

This is where isolated incidents become systems of behaviour.

It is also where many people first realise: *It wasn't random.*

The Psychological Cost of Documentation

(And Why It's Still Necessary)

Documenting harm can feel like re-living it.

There is a cost to that.

Be deliberate about when you document.

Do it once. Do it cleanly. Then step away.

Documentation is not about obsession.

It is about containment.

You are taking what happened out of your body and putting it on the page, where it can be handled rationally later.

That is not a weakness.

That is strategy.

How Documentation Looks in Real Life

Documentation is often imagined as something formal:

a neatly assembled folder produced at the end of a process.

In reality, it is messier, slower, and far more human.

Across Unions A, B, and C, documentation began the same way:

Not with certainty, but with unease.

Each employee sensed something was wrong before they could prove it.

What followed was not a single decisive act.

It was a gradual shift toward recording, preserving, and holding onto fragments that did not yet make sense, but felt important.

Those fragments became receipts.

Union A

Refusing to Outsource the Record

One of the most consequential decisions made by the employee in Union A was this:

The employee did not rely on the employer to keep accurate records.

This was not an act of defiance.

It was an act of realism.

From early on, it became clear that the employer's records were selective: capturing management concerns, omissions, and interpretations, while excluding context, responses, and contradictory material.

Silence was treated as consent.

Absence was treated as failure.

Informal remarks were later elevated to "documented issues."

So the employee kept her own file.

Not as a shadow archive.

As a parallel one.

What the Employee Documented (Independently)

The employee maintained a structured, chronological record that included:

- diary entries noting **dates and times of verbal comments** that were later denied
- follow-up emails sent **after meetings** confirming what had been discussed
- screenshots of **calendar invitations and communications** that contradicted later claims
- copies of **completed work** that was subsequently described as "not done" or "late"
- letters of support obtained contemporaneously, not retrospectively
- drafts of responses saved in sequence, showing how understanding evolved
- statutory declarations prepared **before** outcomes were known
- timelines of events and timelines of work, kept separately

These were not stored haphazardly. They were:

- dated,
- versioned,
- Categorised, and
- preserved

Why This Matters

In contested workplace processes, employers often assume that their file is the file.

It isn't.

An employer's file is a record of what the employer chose to keep.

By maintaining her own archive, the employee ensured that:

- her voice existed independently of management filters
- omissions could be identified, not guessed
- sequence could be demonstrated, not argued

When the employer later asserted that "records do not exist," the employee did not dispute the claim.

The employee simply produced theirs.

The Strategic Advantage of Parallel Records

What this approach neutralised was not just denial, but process manipulation.

It exposed:

- when material had been excluded
- when timelines had been compressed
- when narratives had been constructed after the fact

Most importantly, it prevented the employer from being the sole custodian of reality.

This is not distrust.

This is governance literacy.

A Quiet Truth About Power

Systems that misuse power rely on one assumption:

That workers will trust the system to remember correctly.

The employee from Union A did not make that assumption.

The employee understood something many do not learn until it is too late:

If you do not keep your own record, you may eventually be erased from theirs.

Why This Is Not "Over-Documenting"

Nothing in this record was excessive. It was proportionate to the risk.

The documentation was not created to escalate conflict, but to stabilise truth in an environment where it was already shifting.

That distinction matters.

Union B

Documenting Harm When Power Turns Personal

In Union B, documentation became necessary not because of workload alone, but because the employee was subjected to overlapping forms of harm: professional, psychological, and physical, by multiple actors within the organisation.

Excessive travel demands were only one part of a broader pattern.

What ultimately forced documentation was bullying and harassment by colleagues and supervisors, compounded by sexual harassment, unwanted touching, and assault by a senior executive.

This was not a misunderstanding.

It was not mutual. And it was not subtle.

What The Employee Said: *"I didn't just feel overworked. I felt unsafe."* The employee described an environment where:

- colleagues engaged in bullying behaviours that were normalised as "banter",
- supervisors dismissed concerns or reframed them as resilience issues,
- boundaries were routinely ignored, and
- a Chief of Staff used positional power to sexually harass, touch, and assault her, as documented at the time.

At the time, the employee did not immediately label what was happening as abuse. What the employee felt first was confusion, then fear, then self-doubt.

And finally: the need to record.

What The Employee Documented: Her documentation reflected the reality of layered harm:

- diary entries recording specific incidents of bullying and intimidation
- notes detailing who was present, what was said, and how others reacted
- records of inappropriate comments and sexualised behaviour
- contemporaneous entries documenting unwanted touching and assault
- messages sent to trusted contacts shortly after incidents occurred

- medical records referencing anxiety, panic responses, and trauma symptoms
- calendars and travel records showing the employee was frequently isolated from support
- correspondence where concerns were minimised, deflected, or ignored

What mattered most was timing.
These records were created as events occurred, not reconstructed later.

Why This Documentation Was Essential

Sexual harassment and assault inside workplaces are routinely minimised through:

- disbelief
- delay
- isolation
- procedural avoidance

By the time formal processes are initiated, victims are often asked to recall events that occurred months or years earlier, under scrutiny, scepticism, and emotional strain.

Her documentation disrupted that pattern.

It showed:

- distress recorded in real time
- consistency across different forms of evidence
- escalation following boundary violations
- a clear link between workplace conditions and psychological harm

This was not a story built after exit. It was a record built during survival.

The Role of Power in Silencing

The presence of a Chief of Staff as the perpetrator mattered.

Senior roles carry:

- authority
- credibility
- institutional protection

The employee understood, instinctively, that if her account ever came under challenge, power would speak louder than memory. Documentation was the only counterweight available to her.

Why the Body Became Evidence

As bullying and sexual harassment continued, her body responded before the organisation did.

- Sleep disturbance
- Hypervigilance
- Panic
- Physical shutdown

These symptoms were documented, not because the employee intended to prove anything, but because the employee could no longer function without medical support.

Later, those records became critical.

They showed that harm was not theoretical.

It was embodied.

What Union B Teaches

Union B demonstrates something often missed in workplace narratives:

Harm is rarely singular.

It is cumulative.

It is layered.

And it is often perpetrated by more than one person, across different levels of authority.

Documentation, in this context, was not about strategy.

It was about preserving reality when the environment demanded silence.

Why This Belongs in This Chapter

This chapter is not just about pens and paper.

It is about who controls the story.

In Union B, the employee documented because the alternative was disappearance, not just from the record, but from themselves.

The pen mattered because it gave her something solid to hold onto when everything else was being taken.

Union C

When Sexual Misconduct Allegations Trigger Procedural Collapse

In Union C, documentation revealed a pattern that is both familiar and deeply misunderstood.

The issue was not whether misconduct had occurred.

Nor was it whose account was more credible.

The defining failure was the process itself.

When allegations of sexual misconduct entered the frame, the organisation did not respond with rigour.

It responded with avoidance: procedural, institutional, and strategic.

And importantly, the employee who raised the allegations was male.

The person who perpetrated the abuse was also male.

In his personal life, the perpetrator was in a heterosexual relationship.

This fact was not irrelevant to how the allegations were received.

It introduced a layer of disbelief among those who observed the situation and chose not to intervene.

Not because the allegations were implausible, documentation existed, but because acknowledging them required confronting behaviour that did not align with their assumptions about who commits sexual misconduct, and against whom.

This matters because it exposes a persistent myth: that failures in responding to sexual misconduct are gendered in only one direction.

They are not.

What is gendered is how harm is *explained*.

What is consistent is how institutions protect themselves.

What Happened Next (And What Didn't)

Once allegations involving sexual misconduct were raised, the employee from Union C observed a predictable shift:

- urgency slowed
- scope narrowed
- scrutiny softened
- accountability diffused

Processes that should have become more robust became less so.

Instead of escalation, there was fragmentation.

What He Documented

The employee documented not just events, but institutional behaviour after disclosure:

- timelines showing delays between complaint and response
- requests for clarification that were never answered
- witness lists that were never acted upon
- procedural steps required by policy that were skipped entirely
- investigative terms that avoided sexual misconduct language
- conclusions reached without testing contradictory evidence

Crucially, he documented who decided what and when.

This made it impossible to later claim the failures were accidental.

The conduct documented by the employee did not occur in private or ambiguous settings.

It occurred in public, work-related forums, including major political events and formal workplace functions, in the presence of senior political figures and organisational leaders.

According to the employee's contemporaneous records, the perpetrator, in the company of others including a state government minister, made remarks alleging that the employee was gay, claimed he frequented gay bars in Townsville, used derogatory language, and mocked his prior political associations.

This context is critical.

The presence of high-level politicians and senior figures materially constrained the employee's ability to challenge or confront the behaviour in the moment. Doing so would have required calling out misconduct publicly, in the same forum in which professional reputation, political relationships, and organisational standing were at stake.

This is not incidental.

Public settings with powerful observers often function as informal shields for misconduct, transforming what might otherwise be challenged immediately into behaviour that is deferred, internalised, or later reframed as misunderstanding or banter.

When misconduct occurs in these settings, silence at the time should not be misread as consent, acquiescence, or credibility failure.

It is frequently a rational response to power, visibility, and risk. The procedural failure that followed did not begin after disclosure. It began in the room.

How Procedural Failure Operates After Sexual Misconduct Allegations

Across systems, sexual misconduct allegations often trigger the same institutional reflex:

Minimise risk by minimising process.

This looks like:

- reframing allegations as "interpersonal conflict"
- focusing on conduct outcomes rather than behaviours
- avoiding findings that would trigger mandatory reporting
- narrowing investigations to technical breaches
- concluding matters without evidentiary testing, despite the conduct occurring publicly, in work-related forums attended by senior political figures, where power differentials prevented contemporaneous challenge or correction

None of this requires overt disbelief.

It requires only procedural thinning.

Union C's documentation made visible how procedural thinning replaces scrutiny when power differentials render misconduct socially untouchable.

Why Gender Did Not Protect The Employee

The employee's gender did not shield them.

Nor did it disqualify them.

Instead, it revealed something uncomfortable for institutions:

Sexual misconduct allegations are destabilising to institutions regardless of who raises them.

They threaten:

- leadership credibility
- reputational capital
- governance narratives that legitimise existing power structures

When that threat arises, organisations often prioritise containment over truth.

Union C showed that this response is not about gender.
It is about power preservation.

Absence as Evidence (Again)

Some of the strongest documentation in Union C was negative space:

- no witness interviews
- no trauma-informed process
- no escalation despite policy triggers
- no rationale for procedural shortcuts

These absences were not subtle, accidental, or undocumented.

They were recorded, dated, and aligned against policy requirements.

The employee did not need to argue bias.

They demonstrated breach of process.

This was not a failure of belief.

It was the exercise of power without accountability.

It was an abuse of power.

Why This Pattern Repeats

Institutions struggle with sexual misconduct allegations because they require systems to do three things at once:

1. believe without prejudging
2. investigate without minimising
3. conclude without self-protection

Most fail at step two.

Union C's documentation shows what that failure looks like in real time.

In practice, this failure often looks like retroactive minimisation.

In one comparable case, an employee did not initially recognise the conduct as sexual harassment. The organisation did.

Yet by the time the conduct was named correctly, the outcome had already been determined: the issue was deemed resolved, the perpetrator was temporarily moved, and no disciplinary process followed.

The investigation did not fail because the conduct was unclear. It failed because once the risk was identified, the response shifted to containment rather than accountability.

What Union C Adds to This Chapter

Union C completes the picture begun in Unions A and B.

- Union A documented to prevent narrative manipulation
- Union B documented to survive layered abuse
- Union C documented to expose institutional collapse under pressure

Together, they demonstrate a critical truth:

Sexual misconduct does not break systems. Systems break themselves trying to avoid it.

Before that distinction can matter, one more system behaviour must be named.

In the absence of written evidence, institutions do not remain neutral.

They default to self-protection.

Without documentation, the burden shifts from process to personality.

Accounts are filtered through credibility judgements, rationalisations, and informal defence mechanisms.

Conduct is reframed as misunderstanding.

Harm is softened into awkwardness.

Intent is substituted for impact.

Phrases such as “he didn’t realise what he was doing” or “it was just a joke” do not resolve ambiguity, they close it.

They function as institutional self-defence, insulating both the organisation and the perpetrator from scrutiny, while leaving the affected worker without a record to stand on.

This is why documentation is not simply evidentiary.

It is protective.

Why This Belongs in *The Pen Is Mightier Than the Sword*

This chapter is about more than evidence.

It is about who writes history when harm occurs.

In Union C, the employee understood something vital:

If procedural failure is not documented, it becomes invisible.

If it is invisible, it becomes repeatable.

The pen mattered because it recorded not just what happened, but what should have happened and didn’t.

That distinction is where accountability lives.

Receipts Don’t Always Look Like Evidence

Sometimes, evidence looks like a file structure.

Not a dramatic confrontation.

Not a final report. Just:

- Folders
- Dates
- Versions
- Drafts

In one case, the documentation kept by an employee consisted of nothing more than a steadily growing digital archive. Each folder was named plainly. Each file dated. Nothing hidden. Nothing embellished.

There were folders labelled:

- *Evidence*
- *Return to Work*
- *Rules & Legislation*
- *Operations*
- *Personal File*

Inside them:

- draft statements written and rewritten as clarity evolved
- statutory declarations prepared long before they were needed
- copies of permits, policies, and legislative references
- contemporaneous notes saved not because they were perfect, but because they were timely

At the time, this did not feel powerful. It felt necessary.

This is what documentation often looks like in real life. Quiet. Methodical. Unimpressive to anyone who has never had to defend their own reality. But when narratives later shift, when events are denied, timelines blurred, or records said to be "missing," this kind of archive becomes decisive.

Not because it proves everything. But because it proves consistency. The dates don't move. The file names don't argue.

The versions tell their own story. This is how workers preserve truth when systems rely on forgetfulness.

What This Kind of Evidence Shows (Without Saying a Word)

An archive like this demonstrates:

- the worker anticipated dispute, not because they were malicious, but because they were paying attention
- records were created *before* outcomes were known
- the process unfolded over time, not in hindsight
- documentation was proactive, not reactive

Most importantly, it shows something rarely acknowledged in formal processes:

The worker took the situation seriously long before anyone else did. That matters.

What the Receipts Had in Common

Across all three unions, the documentation shared key characteristics:

- it was factual, not emotive
- it was created close in time to events
- it included confirmation emails after verbal conversations
- it tracked changes in tone and treatment
- it preserved versions before records were altered or disappeared

Crucially, this form of documentation also constrained later character narratives.

Confirmation emails written immediately after verbal conversations recorded clarity, reasonableness, and consistency at the time decisions were made.

Example:

"Thank you for the discussion today regarding my annual leave.

To confirm, we agreed [X] and [Y].

Please let me know if I have misunderstood anything."

The union employees' records did not argue.

They did not persuade, defend, or explain.

They established a timeline, preserved decisions, and recorded not only what happened, but what did not.

In doing so, they exposed omissions the institution could not later explain away.

None of the employees documented with certainty they would "need this one day." They documented because something felt off and they trusted that instinct enough to write it down.

Why This Matters

Receipts do not need to be dramatic to be decisive.

Most cases do not hinge on a single smoking gun.

They hinge on consistency.

Documentation does not shout.

It accumulates.

And when narratives are later rewritten, as they so often are, it provides something rare in these systems:

A fixed point.

A Note on Credibility

All three employees were later subjected to the same tactic:

Their credibility was questioned.

Not because their records were weak, but because their records were strong.

This is why documentation matters.

And this is why it is resisted.

You are not documenting because you expect justice.

You are documenting because truth deserves structure.

A Final Reality Check

You may never need to use your records.

But if you do, you will not regret having them.

People who misuse power rely on:

- memory gaps,
- fatiguc,
- Self-doubt, and
- the hope that you will move on quietly

Documentation removes that advantage.

Documentation also performs a stabilising function.

It externalises events.

Once written down, conduct no longer lives solely in memory, where it can be eroded by repetition, doubt, or minimisation.

The record becomes a reference point outside the system's influence.

That distance matters.

You are not writing to fight.

You are writing to exist on record.

And in systems that depend on silence, that alone is an act of resistance.

By the time people start asking whether they're earning or learning, the documentation already tells a different story.

Part 3
Reclaiming Self

Earning or Learning

THE GATEKEEPER

The Gatekeeper allows you to stay, but not to move. Growth is promised, then endlessly deferred.

RIGHT WITH YOU

If you don't like it, you can leave, but only if we let you go. And we won't.

One of the most frequently repeated justifications in dysfunctional workplaces is the phrase:

"You're either earning or learning."

It is often presented as reassurance.

Even generosity.

If the pay is inadequate, the experience will compensate.

If the conditions are difficult, the lesson will make it worthwhile.

For conscientious, values-driven, or early-career workers, this logic is persuasive. It frames endurance as investment. It keeps people trying. It keeps them staying.

In narcissistic or abusive employment environments, however, this phrase functions less as guidance and more as leverage.

What is rarely acknowledged is that the "learning" never ends, and the "earning" never arrives.

Progress is dangled, then withdrawn.

Development is promised, then redefined.

The worker is told they are fortunate to be where they are, even as their confidence, health, and sense of self quietly erode. In some workplaces, progression is not merely delayed. It is structurally denied.

Advancement is subject to discretionary approval by a single senior authority, with no transparent criteria, no published standards, and no written framework outlining what skills or experience are required to progress.

Workers are told to "develop," yet there is nothing concrete to develop towards. Expectations are implied rather than articulated.

Readiness is assessed subjectively, often retrospectively.

As a result, many employees never progress beyond the level at which they were recruited, regardless of experience, performance, or tenure.

This stagnation is not limited to one role or sector.

In some industries, workers can remain confined within narrow classification bands for years, moving incrementally, if at all, without meaningful advancement.

The appearance of progression is maintained, while actual mobility remains out of reach.

Over time, the absence of standards becomes its own form of control.

When there is no clear pathway, the worker is left to assume that lack of progress reflects a personal deficiency, rather than a system designed to withhold it.

If the worker raises concerns, they are framed as ungrateful.

If they seek growth elsewhere, they are obstructed.

If they attempt to leave, they are suddenly indispensable or quietly sabotaged.

This is not about retaining talent.

It is about controlling narrative.

In many abusive workplaces, this control is subtle. It rarely announces itself through overt threats or explicit prohibitions. Instead, it appears as stalled approvals, mysteriously delayed references, restructures that never quite include you, or sudden "concerns" raised just as opportunities arise.

You may be encouraged to apply for roles, only to be quietly undermined once you do. You may be told you are valued, but never quite supported. You may be assured that your time will come, as long as you remain where you are.

This creates a psychological bind. Staying feels suffocating, but leaving feels dangerous.

Over time, even the idea of movement begins to feel disloyal, risky, or unrealistic. The organisation becomes the gatekeeper not just of your employment, but of your future.

This is how control is maintained without ever being named.

The longer this dynamic persists, the harder it becomes to trust your own perception. You may start to believe that if progress has stalled, it must be because you are lacking, not because the system is invested in your immobility. Self-doubt replaces clarity. Hope is rationed.

By the time you recognise what is happening, the damage has already been normalised.

In these environments, the problem is never framed as the system or the management. It must always be the individual. A successful transition, to another team; another employer; another role, threatens that story. If you thrive elsewhere, it exposes what could not be admitted: that the dysfunction was never you. And that those who maintained it could not tolerate that truth being seen, let alone acknowledged.

That is why you are allowed to stay, but not to go.

It is not that they do not want you.

It is that they do not want anyone else to have you.

This behaviour is often misunderstood as loyalty, concern, or even mentorship. In reality, it reflects insecurity and fear. Fear of exposure, fear of comparison, fear of losing control. The organisation becomes less a place of work and more a closed loop, where your labour is extracted but your growth is contained.

Over time, this containment takes a psychological toll. Many people subjected to these dynamics do not recognise the extent of the harm until years later. The confusion is cumulative. You replay conversations. You question your instincts. You wonder why you feel depleted in a role you were once proud of.

Many people only understand what they have been living through once they are no longer immersed in it. While inside the environment, the constant need to adapt, anticipate, and self-regulate leaves little room for reflection. The nervous system stays alert, scanning for cues, managing risk, and suppressing discomfort in order to function. What feels like resilience is often survival. And survival, once extracted from the environment that demanded it, is rarely recognised as a strength, no matter how much it costs to develop.

When that state finally eases, whether through distance, illness, redundancy, or simple exhaustion, there can be a delayed reckoning.

Memories reorder themselves. Interactions once dismissed as minor begin to carry weight. The body responds before the mind catches up. This is why insight so often arrives later, and why people frequently blame themselves for "not seeing it sooner."

There is no failure in this delay. It is not denial or weakness. It is a predictable response to prolonged constraint. Understanding this is part of reclaiming trust in your own perception and part of letting go of the idea that clarity should have arrived on someone else's timeline.

And because we live in a culture obsessed with productivity, with output; performance metrics; annual reports; economic growth, the harm is easy to dismiss.

You are conditioned to believe that your worth is measured by how much you produce, how much you endure, how adaptable you are to unreasonable conditions.

But this belief is itself part of the trap.

You are not a human doing.

You are a human being.

When identity becomes fused with productivity, stepping away can feel like failure. Many workers internalise the idea that endurance is virtue. That the ability to withstand unreasonable conditions is evidence of strength. In reality, this belief often benefits only the system that imposed the conditions in the first place.

What is presented as loss is rarely loss at all.

Leaving a role that diminishes you is not failure.

Finding work where you are respected is not a retreat.

Being valued, supported, and able to contribute without self-erasure is not a step down.

It is a gain; one the organisation has no incentive to recognise.

That is why departure is reframed as defeat, and why rejection is dressed up as selection: a stronger candidate, a better fit, more experience.

These explanations protect the story. Not the worker.

Rest, distance, and reflection are framed as weakness because they interrupt extraction. Stillness threatens narratives built on sacrifice. And so, people are taught to override their bodies, minimise their distress, and reinterpret harm as "growth."

But learning that costs you your sense of self is not development.

And earning that requires you to disappear is not success.

Reframing work in this way is not about opting out of responsibility or ambition. It is about restoring proportion. Work is one part of a life, not its measure. Employment is a relationship, not a moral verdict.

There will be periods where survival is necessary, where compromise is unavoidable. But those periods are not meant to define you. They are not evidence of who you are or what you deserve.

This understanding often arrives late. Many people only see the pattern once they are removed from it, once the noise subsides and their nervous system begins to settle. What felt like confusion begins to look like coercion. What felt like personal inadequacy begins to resemble systemic misuse.

That realisation can be confronting.

It can also be liberating.

Your value does not come from how much you can tolerate, how much you can fix, or how long you can survive in a system that benefits from your silence.

There are seasons in life where earning matters. There are seasons where learning matters. And there are seasons where neither should come at the cost of your dignity, health, or identity.

This chapter is not written out of malice, nor as an act of revenge disguised as justice. It exists to reframe how you understand what happened and how you understand yourself within it. There are no masks here. But there is a great deal of performance in workplaces that demand loyalty while withholding safety, and resilience while denying humanity.

A workplace genuinely committed to learning does not rely on scarcity or fear to retain people. It invests in training that protects workers in the present, equips them for the future, and remains relevant beyond the organisation itself. People stay not because they must, but because the conditions make staying a rational and voluntary choice.

At some point, the most important thing you can do is stop asking how to make it work and start asking what it has cost you.

What matters most is not how long you stayed, how hard you tried, or how much you endured. What matters is that the story you were given is no longer the one you have to live by.

Leaving, whether physically, psychologically or emotionally, is not a failure of resilience. It is often the first act of it. Choosing distance is not giving up. It is reclaiming authorship over your own life.

The systems that benefit from your self-doubt will always frame your departure as loss: theirs or yours.

But clarity is not a loss.

Rest is not a loss.

Integrity is not a loss.

At some point, learning becomes remembering who you were before the confusion began. And earning becomes something broader than income: the quiet return of trust in yourself.

That is not a weakness.

That is not a retreat.

That is the work.

With distance comes clarity. Once you stop trying to survive inside the system, patterns that once felt personal begin to reveal themselves as structural.

Behaviours repeat.

Justifications echo.

Outcomes follow a familiar script.

What once felt chaotic starts to look organised, not in intent perhaps, but in effect.

This is often the moment that unsettles people the most.

Because recognising a pattern means accepting that what happened was neither isolated nor accidental.

It also means accepting that understanding comes before resolution.

Before accountability.

Before any meaningful sense of justice.

The next step is not action.

It is recognition.

Naming what has already shown itself.

Calmly, carefully, and without distortion, so that it no longer holds power through confusion alone.

Now is not the time to prove anything.

Now is not the time to justify your value.

Now is your time to just be.

Naming The Patterns

THE ARCHIVIST

The Archivist brings order to confusion.
They name what repeats and strip chaos of its disguise.
Understanding begins here.

RIGHT WITH YOU

From Confusion to Coherence

Confusion is often the first signal that something is wrong, though it is rarely recognised as such at the time.

In unhealthy workplaces, confusion does not arise from a lack of intelligence or resilience on the part of the worker.

It arises because the environment itself is inconsistent by design.

When expectations shift without explanation, when feedback contradicts prior guidance, when behaviour is rewarded one day and questioned the next, people naturally look inward for the explanation. They assume they have misunderstood, misstepped, or failed to adapt.

This reflex is human. It is also convenient for systems that benefit from keeping scrutiny individual rather than collective.

Naming patterns is not about labelling people or assigning motives. It is about restoring coherence. Once experiences are placed in context, they stop feeling random.

What once felt personal begins to look structural. And what once felt like chaos begins to follow a recognisable logic.

This chapter is about that logic, and the patterns that sustain it.

Pattern One: Shifting Standards

One of the most destabilising features of a dysfunctional workplace is the absence of stable standards.

Expectations exist, but they are not fixed. Goals are set, then quietly revised. Instructions are given, then later denied. What is required is never fully articulated, yet failure to meet it is keenly felt.

In these environments, workers often find themselves chasing an invisible target. When one benchmark is met, another appears. When a task is completed as requested, the criteria change. Feedback arrives late, vaguely framed, or retrospectively applied. Success is never quite acknowledged, but shortcomings are meticulously noted.

This pattern keeps people perpetually off balance. Because the rules are unclear, effort increases. People work harder, stay later, over-prepare, and second-guess themselves in an attempt to anticipate expectations that are never fully disclosed. The problem is framed as one of adaptability: if only you were more flexible, more intuitive, more aligned.

Over time, this erodes confidence.

The worker begins to doubt their judgement, even in areas where they were once competent.

The constant adjustment required leaves little room for reflection or self-trust.

Importantly, this instability is often defended as dynamism or high standards, when in reality it prevents accountability. Standards that cannot be pinned down cannot be questioned.

Over time, this instability does more than exhaust individuals. It quietly fractures collectives. When standards are unclear and success is scarce, comparison replaces collaboration. Workers begin to measure themselves against one another rather than against a shared set of expectations. Competition emerges where none is required, not because people are ambitious, but because uncertainty creates fear. In this way, shifting standards do the work of division without ever naming it. People turn inward, and sometimes against each other, doing on the organisation's behalf, what it no longer needs to enforce directly.

Pattern Two: Narrative Control

Alongside shifting standards sits another, quieter mechanism: narrative control.

In many organisations, the story about what is happening matters as much as, or more than, what is actually happening. How events are framed, who is described as "difficult," "resilient," "committed," or "concerning," shapes outcomes long before any formal process begins.

Narratives are rarely imposed outright.

They are suggested, reinforced, and repeated in subtle ways.

Concerns are raised "informally." Observations are shared "in confidence."

Context is selectively included or omitted.

Over time, these fragments merge into an accepted version of events.

For the person at the centre of this narrative, the effect can be deeply disorienting.

You may recognise yourself less and less in the way you are described.

Your intentions are reframed.

Your reactions are taken as evidence of disposition rather than response.

Attempts to clarify are interpreted as defensiveness.

Silence is read as confirmation.

This is not simply miscommunication. It is a form of containment.

When the narrative is controlled, outcomes appear inevitable rather than constructed. Decisions seem neutral, even when they consistently disadvantage the same individuals. The story becomes self-justifying.

Pattern Three: Isolation Through Process

Isolation in unhealthy workplaces is rarely overt. It does not require exclusion or hostility. More often, it is achieved through process.

Formal mechanisms that are ostensibly designed to support: performance management; complaints procedures; wellbeing initiatives, can, in practice, separate people from one another. Concerns are handled individually. Conversations are compartmentalised. Information is siloed.

Each person is encouraged to focus on their own behaviour, their own response, their own resilience. Structural similarities between experiences remain unspoken. People who might otherwise compare notes are kept apart by confidentiality requirements, procedural timelines, or simple exhaustion.

This isolation is reinforced by the language of professionalism. Discussing concerns is framed as inappropriate. Seeking validation is discouraged. Trusting one's own perception is subtly undermined. Over time, individuals come to believe that whatever they are experiencing must be unique: a personal failure rather than a shared condition.

The result is loneliness within a crowd. People work side by side while feeling profoundly alone in their doubts.

The system remains unchallenged, not because harm is absent, but because connection is interrupted.

For many, recognition arrives, not during conflict, but during moments of supposed belonging: a meeting, a team gathering, a room full of colleagues, when the absence of connection becomes undeniable.

Pattern Four: Inversion of Responsibility

Perhaps the most damaging pattern is the inversion of responsibility, the quiet shifting of accountability away from systems and onto individuals.

In this dynamic, harm is reframed as sensitivity. Burnout becomes a capacity issue. Distress is treated as a personal vulnerability rather than a predictable response to sustained pressure. Those who struggle are encouraged to access support, build resilience, or adjust their mindset.

While support is not inherently problematic, it becomes so when it replaces examination of the conditions that made it necessary. Responsibility moves downward. The question is no longer "What is happening here?" but "Why aren't you coping?"

This inversion can be difficult to detect, particularly for people who are conscientious and self-reflective.

They take feedback seriously.

They are willing to improve.

When told they are the issue, they look for ways to fix themselves.

This dynamic is intensified when individuals observe that others are not held to the same standard. Peers who refuse accountability, deflect responsibility, or show no interest in self-reflection remain unchallenged, while those who engage honestly with feedback are scrutinised more closely. The resulting disparity creates resentment and anger, not as character flaws, but as predictable responses to injustice. When those reactions surface, they are then cited as further evidence of the individual's unsuitability: proof that they are not a "team player," not aligned, not a good fit, even as genuine teamwork, shared accountability, and collective responsibility are notably absent.

What is lost in this process is proportion. Systems with disproportionate power are treated as neutral. Individuals with limited power are treated as responsible for outcomes beyond their control. Over time, this distorts self-perception and entrenches self-blame.

Pattern Five: The Erosion of Self-Trust

One of the least visible consequences of these environments is the gradual erosion of self-trust. This does not happen through a single incident or overt act. It happens incrementally, through repeated moments where instinct is overridden, perception is questioned, and judgement is subtly displaced.

When feedback is inconsistent and responsibility is continually redirected inward, people learn to doubt their own reading of situations. They stop relying on their internal compass and begin to look outward for cues: approval, reassurance, correction. Decisions that once felt straightforward now require excessive checking. Confidence gives way to caution.

This erosion is often mistaken for humility or professionalism. In reality, it is a form of adaptation. When environments are unpredictable, people become hyper-vigilant. They monitor tone, anticipate reactions, and adjust themselves in advance of feedback that may or may not come. Over time, this self-monitoring becomes habitual.

What makes this particularly damaging is that it disguises itself as insight. People believe they are becoming more self-aware, more reflective, more accountable. In fact, they are becoming less anchored in their own experience. The line between genuine self-examination and imposed self-doubt becomes blurred.

Self-reflection continues, but it is no longer guided by personal values or internal judgement.

It is conducted within the invisible limits set by the organisation, where insight is permitted only insofar as it aligns with external expectations.

This loss of self-trust has lasting effects beyond the workplace. Even after leaving, people may second-guess decisions, minimise discomfort, or dismiss early warning signs. Rebuilding trust in one's own perception takes time and it often begins only once the pattern is named.

Recognising this erosion is not an exercise in blame. It is an act of orientation. Understanding how self-trust was undermined allows it to be rebuilt deliberately, rather than expected to return on its own.

When Patterns Overlap

These patterns rarely operate in isolation. More often, they overlap and reinforce one another.

Shifting standards create confusion.

Narrative control explains the confusion away.

Isolation prevents shared understanding.

Inverted responsibility ensures the system remains intact.

For those inside it, the experience can feel like walking on unstable ground, never quite sure where the next step will land.

The effort required to remain functional absorbs energy that might otherwise be used for reflection or challenge.

This is why recognition often arrives later. Not because the signs were absent, but because the environment discouraged seeing them clearly.

Recognition as Stabilisation

Naming patterns is not about reliving the past. It is about removing confusion from the present.

When experiences are understood in context, they lose much of their power to disorient. What once felt like personal inadequacy begins to look like a predictable response to unstable conditions. What once felt like failure begins to look like information.

This recognition can be unsettling.

It asks people to revise stories they have told themselves.

Stories about strength, endurance, loyalty, and responsibility.

But it can also be grounding.

Clarity restores proportion.

It allows distance where there was once entanglement.

Importantly, recognition does not require immediate action. It does not demand confrontation or resolution. It simply asks for honesty, with oneself first.

Understanding the pattern is not the end of the process.

It is the beginning of a more accurate accounting.

And before any assessment of cost, consequence, or next steps can be made, that accuracy matters.

The next chapter turns to what prolonged exposure to these patterns takes from a person, not in dramatic terms, but in quiet, cumulative ways that are often overlooked until long after the fact.

The Cost of Staying

THE ENDURER

**The Endurer keeps going.
What looks like resilience is
prolonged exposure.
By the time the cost is visible, it
has already been paid.**

RIGHT WITH YOU

The Myth of "Just Getting Through

The cost of staying is rarely obvious while it is being paid. There is no single moment that announces itself as the point of harm, no clear threshold beyond which damage is undeniable. Instead, the impact accumulates quietly, through ordinary days and reasonable compromises made repeatedly.

Most people do not remain in unhealthy environments because they fail to recognise harm. They stay because they believe it is temporary, manageable, or necessary. They tell themselves they can endure a little longer, that the situation will stabilise, that leaving would be disproportionate to what they are experiencing.

This belief is often reinforced by the absence of a clear crisis. Nothing is "bad enough." Nothing quite justifies disruption.

The language of endurance plays a powerful role here.

Getting through becomes a virtue.

Pushing on is reframed as resilience.

Discomfort is minimised, contextualised, or deferred.

Each day feels survivable on its own, even as the overall toll grows heavier.

What makes this particularly insidious is that the harm does not arrive as a sudden decline.

It arrives as an adaptation.

The nervous system recalibrates.

The mind narrows its focus.

Energy is redirected toward coping rather than living.

Over time, this state begins to feel normal, not because it is healthy, but because it has become familiar.

The myth of "just getting through" relies on the idea that there will eventually be a moment of relief, a point at which effort is rewarded and equilibrium restored. But in environments that rely on prolonged strain, that moment rarely comes. What changes instead is the person's capacity, not upward, but inward. Expectations are lowered. Boundaries soften. What once felt unacceptable begins to feel inevitable.

By the time people question the cost, they often do so quietly, almost apologetically. They wonder if they are overreacting, if others would cope better, if leaving would mean they failed to endure what was simply part of working life. These questions are not signs of weakness. They are evidence of how thoroughly endurance has been normalised.

This chapter begins here because the cost of staying is not paid all at once.

It is paid in increments small enough to ignore, until they are not.

The Cognitive Cost

One of the earliest costs of prolonged exposure is cognitive, though it is rarely recognised as such. Thinking does not stop, but it changes. Attention narrows. Decisions that were once made with ease begin to require disproportionate effort. Mental energy is consumed, not by the work itself, but by managing uncertainty around it.

In unstable environments, people spend significant cognitive effort anticipating change. They scan for cues, monitor tone, replay conversations, and prepare contingencies. What appears from the outside as overthinking is often a rational response to inconsistency. When rules shift and expectations are unclear, vigilance becomes a survival strategy.

Over time, this vigilance becomes exhausting. Decision-making slows, not because capacity is lost, but because every choice carries additional weight. Even minor actions are evaluated for potential consequence. People hesitate, seek reassurance, or delay decisions they once would have made instinctively. Confidence gives way to caution.

Another subtle cost is the erosion of mental bandwidth. Cognitive resources are finite. When a significant portion is devoted to self-monitoring and risk management, less remains for creativity, strategic thinking, or long-term planning. People may notice that their thinking feels flatter, more literal, less expansive than it once did. Ideas feel harder to access. Perspective narrows.

This cognitive narrowing is often misinterpreted as decline. Individuals may worry that they are becoming less capable or less sharp. In reality, their minds are overloaded, not diminished. The constant demand to adapt to unstable conditions leaves little space for reflection or recovery.

Importantly, this change is rarely abrupt. It unfolds gradually, making it difficult to identify a clear starting point. People adapt to the new baseline without noticing the shift.

Only later, often after distance is achieved, does the contrast become clear. What once felt like a personal failing is recognised as the cost of sustained cognitive strain.

Understanding this cost matters because it reframes the experience. Difficulty concentrating, indecision, and mental fatigue are not signs of inadequacy. They are predictable outcomes of prolonged exposure to environments that require constant adjustment without offering stability in return.

The Emotional Cost

The emotional cost of staying is often the hardest to articulate, not because it is insignificant, but because it develops quietly and resists simple language. Unlike acute distress, which demands attention, this cost accumulates gradually, reshaping emotional life in ways that can be difficult to notice while they are happening.

In prolonged environments of instability, emotional expression narrows. People learn which feelings are acceptable and which are not. Frustration must be moderated. Disappointment must be managed privately. Anger is reframed as unprofessional. Over time, this selective expression becomes internalised. Emotions are filtered before they are fully felt.

This process does not necessarily result in heightened distress. More often, it produces emotional flattening. The range of feeling contracts. Joy becomes muted. Relief is brief. Even positive experiences are experienced cautiously, as though they might be withdrawn without notice. What develops is not constant sadness, but a kind of emotional holding pattern.

Another cost is the gradual loss of emotional safety. When reactions are monitored or misinterpreted, people stop trusting that their inner experience will be received accurately. They begin to second-guess their responses: Am I being unreasonable? Too sensitive? Overreacting?

This self-questioning shifts attention away from what is being felt toward how it will be perceived.

Over time, emotional energy is redirected toward regulation rather than expression. People become adept at containing themselves, smoothing over discomfort, and maintaining composure. While this may appear as emotional maturity, it often comes at the expense of authenticity. Feelings are managed rather than integrated.

This containment can extend beyond the workplace. Emotional reserve becomes habitual. People may find themselves less expressive in relationships, less responsive to pleasure, or less able to access grief and anger when those emotions are appropriate. The emotional self becomes guarded, not out of choice, but out of prolonged necessity.

Like the cognitive cost, the emotional cost is rarely recognised while it is accruing. It is only when emotional range begins to return, often after distance or safety is restored, that the extent of what was lost becomes clear. What felt like composure is revealed as suppression. What feels like strength is understood as endurance.

Naming this cost is not about pathologising emotional adaptation. It is about recognising that emotions narrowed for a reason and that widening them again takes time, safety, and permission.

The Physical / Somatic Cost

The physical cost of staying is often the least acknowledged, even as it is one of the most enduring.

This is partly because the body adapts quietly, and partly because physical symptoms are easier to rationalise as unrelated, temporary, or inevitable.

Prolonged exposure to unstable environments places the nervous system under sustained strain.

The body remains in a state of readiness: alert, responsive, braced. Over time, this heightened state becomes the baseline. What begins as a stress response settles into the background of daily life.

Sleep is often the first casualty. Rest becomes lighter, more fragmented. People wake feeling unrefreshed, as though recovery never quite completes. Tension accumulates in the body: in the jaw, shoulders, neck, or lower back and is carried without conscious notice. Headaches, gastrointestinal issues, and unexplained fatigue are common, yet easily dismissed.

Because these symptoms fluctuate, they are rarely linked directly to the environment causing them. A better week suggests improvement. A quieter period offers false reassurance. People tell themselves they are coping, even as their bodies continue to absorb strain.

Another cost is the gradual loss of bodily awareness. When attention is directed outward, toward anticipating demands and managing risk, signals from the body are deprioritised. Hunger, exhaustion, and pain are overridden in the service of functioning. Over time, people become less attuned to early warning signs and more accustomed to pushing through discomfort.

This disconnection can persist long after the environment itself is left behind. The body may continue to respond as though threat remains, even when circumstances have changed. Relaxation feels unfamiliar. Stillness can be unsettling. Recovery is not immediate, because the body has learned to expect pressure.

Understanding the somatic cost is not about attributing every physical symptom to work. It is about recognising that the body participates fully in prolonged exposure, even when harm is not dramatic or visible. Strain does not need to be catastrophic to be real.

Re-establishing physical equilibrium takes time. It requires safety, consistency, and patience, not because the body is broken, but because it has adapted well to conditions that asked too much of it for too long.

The Relational Cost

The relational cost of staying often unfolds quietly, at the edges of daily life. It is not marked by conflict or rupture, but by gradual withdrawal. Energy that might once have been available for connection is redirected toward coping, leaving less capacity for presence, openness, or ease with others.

In prolonged environments of strain, people become selective about what they share. Experiences are difficult to explain, and responses can feel unpredictable. Concerns are minimised to avoid burdening others or inviting misunderstanding.

Over time, this self-censorship becomes habitual. Silence begins to feel safer than explanation.

Another relational cost is the erosion of trust in being understood. When one's experiences are repeatedly questioned, reframed, or dismissed in a professional context, it becomes harder to believe that they will be received differently elsewhere. People may find themselves bracing for disbelief or advice when what they need is recognition. This anticipation can inhibit togetherness.

Relationships may also be affected by emotional availability. As emotional range narrows and energy is conserved, people may appear distant or preoccupied. Loved ones may sense the change without fully understanding its cause. The distance is rarely intentional, but it can still be felt.

There is also a subtler cost related to shame. When difficulty is internalised as personal inadequacy, people may withdraw to protect their self-image.

They avoid conversations that might expose vulnerability or invite comparison. What was once shared openly becomes private, then unspoken.

Over time, these patterns can alter how people relate more broadly. Connection becomes challenging. Asking for support feels uncomfortable. Receiving care may trigger unease rather than relief. The relational world contracts, not from disinterest, but from sustained self-protection.

Like the other costs described here, the relational cost often becomes visible only in retrospect. When safety returns, people may notice how much connection was postponed or muted. Rebuilding trust, in others and in being met, is part of the recovery that follows prolonged exposure.

Why the Cost Is Often Seen Too Late

The cost of staying is rarely recognised in real time, because it does not announce itself as damage. It presents instead as adaptation. People adjust, recalibrate, and compensate in ways that allow them to continue functioning, often at a level that appears outwardly competent or even successful.

This adaptation can be convincing. When performance is maintained, it becomes harder to justify concern. When responsibilities are met, strain is reframed as normal pressure. When others appear to cope, comparison reinforces silence. The absence of a visible breaking point creates the illusion that no harm is being done.

Another reason the cost is seen late is that the effects are distributed across time and domains. Cognitive fatigue, emotional narrowing, physical tension, and relational withdrawal rarely peak simultaneously. They appear in fragments, easily attributed to circumstance, age, or temperament. Without a single cause to point to, the pattern remains obscured.

Distance plays a critical role in recognition.

Only when the environment changes: through leaving, illness, redundancy, or enforced pause, does contrast become possible. What once felt manageable is revealed as constraining. What once felt like personal limitation begins to look like sustained exposure.

There is often grief in this recognition.

Not only for what was endured, but for what was postponed: ease, connection, creativity, health.

People may wish they had understood sooner, spoken earlier, left faster.

These reflections are understandable, but misplaced. Clarity does not arrive on demand. It arrives when conditions allow.

Understanding why the cost was seen late is not about assigning fault to oneself. It is about restoring proportion. Prolonged exposure alters perception. Endurance blurs boundaries. Seeing clearly again is not failure. It is evidence that the conditions have changed.

This chapter closes the accounting, not to dwell on loss, but to make the next question possible.

Once the cost is understood, staying is no longer the default.

What comes next is not driven by urgency, but by choice.

Letting Go

THE RELEASER

**The Releaser chooses distance.
Not out of defeat,
but discernment.
What is released no longer
controls.**

RIGHT WITH YOU

The Shift from Endurance

Letting go is rarely a single decision. More often, it begins as a subtle internal shift: a moment when endurance stops feeling like strength and starts feeling like cost. Nothing dramatic changes on the surface. The work may continue. The structure may remain. But the internal calculation alters.

For a long time, survival has been the organising principle. Energy has been directed toward coping, adapting, and maintaining equilibrium in conditions that require constant adjustment. Endurance became a way of staying intact. It was necessary, and at times it was the only available option.

The shift occurs when survival is no longer enough.

This moment does not arrive with certainty or confidence. It often arrives quietly, as a question rather than a conclusion:

What if I didn't have to keep doing this?

The question may feel disloyal, unrealistic, or premature. It may be dismissed repeatedly before it is taken seriously.

What changes is not resolve, but orientation. Instead of asking how much longer one can endure, attention turns toward what is being endured, and more importantly, why. The focus moves from tolerating conditions to evaluating them. Survival gives way to discernment.

This shift can be unsettling. Endurance provides structure. It offers a sense of purpose, even when it extracts a high price. Letting go of survival as the primary strategy can feel like stepping into uncertainty without armour.

But this is also where choice begins to re-emerge.

Choice does not require immediate action. It does not demand answers or timelines. At first, it simply allows space for honesty. About limits, desire, and what can no longer be justified as temporary or necessary.

This chapter is not about decisive exits or clean breaks. It is about recognising the moment when endurance stops being adaptive, and choice becomes possible.

What Feels at Risk When Endurance Ends

When survival has been the organising principle for a long time, the idea of letting go can feel destabilising, not because the current situation is good, but because it is known. Endurance, however costly, provides structure. It answers the question of what to do each day. It offers a role to inhabit.

When that role begins to loosen, a different question emerges:

If I stop enduring this, what do I lose?

The answers are rarely limited to income or status, though those concerns matter. What often feels most at risk is identity. People who have survived prolonged strain frequently define themselves by their capacity to cope. They are the reliable one, the steady one, the person who keeps going when things are difficult.

Letting go of endurance can feel like letting go of that self-concept.

There is also fear around legitimacy. If staying requires so much effort, then choosing not to stay can feel like an admission that the effort was misplaced. People may worry that leaving reframes their past endurance as unnecessary or naïve. This fear can keep them anchored long after the original justification has faded.

Another risk is uncertainty. Survival narrows focus. Choice opens it. When the future is no longer dictated by immediate demands, possibilities reappear, and with them, ambiguity. For people who have lived under sustained pressure, uncertainty can feel more threatening than known difficulty.

There is often fear of judgement as well. Others may not understand the internal shift. From the outside, letting go can appear sudden or unjustified. The absence of a visible crisis invites questions that are hard to answer succinctly. Explaining prolonged exposure to someone who has not lived it can feel exhausting, or futile.

These fears are not signs that letting go is wrong. They are predictable responses to a long period in which endurance was necessary. Survival strategies do not dissolve simply because conditions change. They recede gradually, as safety and trust are re-established.

Recognising what feels at risk allows choice to be approached with honesty rather than force.

It clarifies why letting go is rarely immediate and why it often unfolds in stages, long before any external change is visible.

How Choice Begins to Reappear

Choice rarely returns all at once. After a long period of survival, it tends to reappear tentatively, in small internal shifts rather than visible actions. These early expressions of choice are easy to overlook because they do not look decisive. They look quiet, even hesitant.

One of the first signs is a change in internal language. People stop automatically justifying what they are enduring. The explanations that once came easily: it's only temporary, this is just how it is, I can manage, begin to feel thin. Not false exactly, but incomplete. The mind no longer rushes to defend the situation against its own discomfort.

Another sign is the return of preference. After prolonged exposure, many people lose touch with what they want because wanting feels impractical or irrelevant. As choice begins to re-emerge, preference surfaces in modest ways: a desire for more predictability, more rest, more respect, more time. These desires are not yet planned. They are signals.

Choice also shows up as boundary awareness. People begin to notice what drains them disproportionately and what restores them, even slightly. They may still comply with demands, but with a growing awareness of cost. What once passed unnoticed now registers. This noticing is not resentment. It is information.

Importantly, early choice often remains internal. People may not share it. They may not act on it. They may not even fully trust it yet. That is appropriate. After endurance, trust in one's own judgement needs to be rebuilt gradually. Choice strengthens through repetition, not declaration.

This stage can feel frustrating, because it lacks momentum. There is insight without resolution, and awareness without movement. But this is not stagnation. It is recalibration. Just as survival narrowed focus, the re-emergence of choice widens it slowly, allowing room for discernment.

Before choice becomes visible, it becomes imaginable. That shift, from I have to, toward I could, marks a profound internal change. It signals that survival is no longer the only strategy in play, even if it remains temporarily necessary.

The Pressure to Act and the Value of Restraint

Once choice begins to reappear, it is often accompanied by a new and unexpected pressure: the sense that something must now be done.

Insight creates momentum, and momentum can feel urgent. People may worry that if they do not act quickly, the clarity they have gained will be lost.

This pressure does not usually come from within alone. It is reinforced by cultural narratives that equate awareness with action and decisiveness with strength.

Having recognised a harmful situation, people are encouraged, implicitly or explicitly, to resolve it, leave it, confront it, or transcend it. Waiting can be mistaken for fear. Caution can be misread as avoidance.

For those emerging from prolonged survival, this pressure can be destabilising.

Survival required constant response to external demands.

Acting too quickly after that period risks replacing one form of reactivity with another.

Choice becomes something to perform rather than inhabit.

Restraint at this stage is not passivity.

It is discernment.

It allows insight to settle, preferences to clarify, and internal authority to strengthen.

Acting before this internal grounding is established can recreate familiar dynamics: urgency, justification, over-explanation, even when the decision itself is sound.

There is also a practical dimension to restraint. Leaving, changing direction, or asserting boundaries often carries consequences. Rushing into action without adequate support, resources, or preparation can compound stress rather than relieve it. Allowing time for choice to mature reduces the likelihood that decisions will be shaped primarily by exhaustion or relief-seeking.

Importantly, restraint restores agency. Survival is characterised by necessity, while restraint reintroduces deliberateness. It affirms that action will occur not because pressure demands it, but because it aligns with one's values and capacity.

Letting choice breathe is part of letting go. It honours the fact that recovery from prolonged endurance is not linear and does not benefit from being rushed.

Movement that follows this period tends to be steadier, clearer, and more sustainable, because it is chosen, not compelled.

What Letting Go Often Looks Like

Letting go is often imagined as a decisive act: a resignation, a confrontation, a clear turning point. In reality, it more often unfolds as a series of small disengagements, many of which are invisible to others and sometimes even to the person experiencing them.

One of the earliest signs is emotional decoupling. People begin to invest less of themselves in outcomes they no longer control or believe in. They still perform their roles, but with clearer limits. What once felt personal starts to feel contextual. This is not apathy. It is the proportion returning.

Another sign is the quiet withdrawal of justification. Explanations that were once offered automatically: to colleagues, to loved ones, to oneself, are no longer rehearsed. There is less need to convince, defend, or normalise. Silence replaces explanation, not out of secrecy, but out of clarity.

Letting go can also appear as a change in attention. Energy shifts away from managing impressions and toward preserving wellbeing. People may stop volunteering for additional responsibilities, disengage from unproductive dynamics, or decline opportunities that once felt obligatory.

These decisions are rarely announced. They are enacted quietly.

In some cases, letting go involves physical departure: leaving a role, an organisation, or a situation. In others, it involves psychological distance while external circumstances remain unchanged for a time.

Both forms are valid.

Letting go is not defined by visibility, but by internal alignment.

Importantly, letting go does not always feel relieving at first.

There can be sadness, uncertainty, and even grief for what was hoped for but did not materialise.

These emotions do not mean the decision is wrong.

They reflect the complexity of releasing something that once mattered.

What distinguishes letting go from resignation is agency. Resignation collapses possibility. Letting go restores it. One closes the future down, the other opens it cautiously. Letting go makes room, not immediately for answers, but for breath.

Choice as an Ongoing Practice

Choice, once it reappears, is rarely resolved in a single moment. It is not a declaration made once and then completed.

More often, it becomes a practice: something returned to repeatedly as circumstances, capacity, and understanding evolve.

After prolonged survival, it can be tempting to look for a final decision that will restore certainty: the moment of leaving, the correct path forward, the action that proves endurance is over.

But this expectation can recreate the same pressure that made survival necessary in the first place. Choice does not need to be absolute to be real.

Practiced choice shows up in how people allocate energy, how they respond to demands, and how they assess what they owe, and to whom. It appears in small refusals, in pauses before agreement, in the willingness to reconsider what was once taken for granted.

These moments may seem insignificant, but they accumulate.

What makes choice sustainable is that it remains responsive rather than rigid.

It allows for revision without self-betrayal. It recognises that clarity deepens over time, and that decisions made with care can be adjusted without being invalidated.

Importantly, choice does not require justification. One of the lasting effects of prolonged endurance is the belief that decisions must be defended to be legitimate. Practicing choice gently unravels this belief. It affirms that consent matters, not only in beginnings, but in continuations.

This chapter marks the point at which survival is no longer the default setting.

What follows is not certainty, but agency. Not resolution, but direction. Choice restores movement without demanding haste.

The chapters that follow will explore what becomes possible once endurance is no longer the organising principle: how power is reclaimed, how voice returns, and how a life shaped by necessity can begin to be authored deliberately.

Reclaiming Agency

THE SOVEREIGN

The Sovereign governs themselves. They no longer seek permission, validation, or approval. Authority is internal. Choice is deliverate.

RIGHT WITH YOU

When Power Returns Quietly

Reclaiming agency does not announce itself.

It does not arrive with confidence, certainty, or a visible shift in circumstances.

More often, it begins as an internal reorientation: a quiet return of authority over one's own attention, energy, and decisions.

For a long time, power was experienced externally.

Decisions were shaped by necessity, response, and constraint. Attention was directed outward: toward demands, expectations, and consequences.

Agency was not absent, but it was limited, exercised within narrow margins.

When endurance loosens its grip, something subtle changes.

People begin to notice where their energy goes and where it no longer needs to go.

They stop reacting automatically.

They pause.

The pause itself becomes an expression of power.

This form of agency can feel unfamiliar because it lacks drama.

There is no confrontation, no declaration, no visible victory. In cultures that equate power with dominance or assertion, quiet authority is easy to overlook. But it is often more durable.

Agency at this stage is not about influencing others.

It is about self-alignment.

Decisions are made with less reference to external approval and more reference to internal coherence. People begin to trust their sense of proportion again: what matters, what doesn't, what is worth engaging with, and what is not.

This return of power can feel fragile at first.

After prolonged exposure to environments that demanded compliance or adaptation, asserting internal authority may trigger doubt.

Am I allowed to do this?

Is this reasonable?

These questions are not signs of weakness; they are echoes of a time when agency carried risk.

What changes gradually is the answer.

Permission is no longer sought externally. It is generated internally, through repetition and consistency. Agency strengthens, not through assertion, but through practice.

This chapter is about that practice: the quiet, often invisible ways power begins to return once survival is no longer the organising principle.

Agency Is Not Control

After prolonged exposure to coercive or unstable environments, it is easy to confuse agency with control. This is understandable. When power has been constrained, the instinct is often to compensate by trying to manage outcomes more tightly; to anticipate, direct, or secure certainty where it was previously denied. But agency does not require control over others, events, or systems.

In fact, the two are often in tension. Control seeks to eliminate uncertainty. Agency accepts uncertainty and locates authority within one's own responses to it.

This distinction matters because many people emerging from prolonged endurance carry habits that were once protective, but are no longer necessary.

Hyper-vigilance, over-preparation, and constant contingency planning can persist even when the original threat has passed.

These behaviours may feel like empowerment, but they often keep the nervous system locked in a state of readiness.

Agency, by contrast, is characterised by selectivity.

It involves choosing where to engage and where not to. It allows outcomes to unfold without constant intervention. Rather than attempting to manage everything, agency clarifies what belongs to you and what does not.

This shift can feel risky at first. Letting go of control may resemble passivity or neglect, particularly for those who have learned that vigilance was required to avoid harm. But agency is not indifference.

It is discernment. Importantly, agency restores proportionality. Not every issue requires a response. Not every injustice must be addressed personally. Not every misalignment needs to be corrected. Choosing not to engage is as much an expression of power as choosing to act.

Understanding agency as distinct from control allows people to step out of reactive patterns without abandoning responsibility. It reframes power as something exercised internally, through boundaries and choices, rather than externally, through force or persuasion. This distinction creates space for a different kind of strength; one that is quieter, steadier, and less draining.

Why Agency Can Feel Uncomfortable

Reclaiming agency often brings discomfort, even when it is clearly needed. This discomfort can be confusing. After all, agency is associated with autonomy, strength, and relief. Yet for many people emerging from prolonged constraint, exercising agency can feel unfamiliar, exposed, or even unsafe.

One reason for this unease is that agency disrupts established roles. In environments shaped by endurance and adaptation, people learn who they are allowed to be: reliable, accommodating, resilient. When behaviour changes, when responses slow, boundaries firm, or engagement becomes selective, it can unsettle others' expectations. This shift may be met with confusion, resistance, or subtle pushback.

There is also internal discomfort. After long periods of orienting around external demands, internal authority can feel tentative. Decisions may trigger doubt rather than confidence. People may wonder whether they are being unreasonable, selfish, or overly cautious. These questions are not signs that agency is misplaced. They are echoes of earlier conditioning.

Another source of discomfort is the absence of immediate feedback. Survival strategies are reinforced quickly: comply and the pressure eases, adapt and the conflict subsides. Agency does not always offer such immediate relief. Boundaries may hold tension rather than resolve it. Choosing not to engage may feel awkward rather than satisfying. This delayed reinforcement can make agency feel less rewarding at first.

Agency can also surface grief. As people assert choice, they may recognise how little choice they previously had, or how much was compromised to maintain stability. This recognition can be painful. It brings into focus what was deferred or surrendered during prolonged endurance. Feeling this grief does not undermine agency. It accompanies it.

Understanding why agency feels uncomfortable helps prevent misinterpretation. Discomfort does not mean something is wrong. Often, it signals that a familiar pattern is loosening. Over time, as agency is practised and reinforced, the discomfort softens. What once felt risky begins to feel proportionate. What once felt foreign becomes familiar.

Reclaiming agency is not about eliminating unease. It is about learning to move with it and steadily, without retreating into old patterns of self-suppression.

Power Without Replicating the Old Hierarchy

One of the quiet risks that can emerge during recovery is the temptation to reclaim power by mirroring the very dynamics that once caused harm. After prolonged constraint, it can feel validating to assert dominance, control outcomes, or correct others forcefully. These impulses are understandable. They arise from a desire to ensure that one is never again placed in a position of powerlessness.

But agency does not require the replication of hierarchy. Power reclaimed through domination remains tethered to the same framework that enabled coercion in the first place. It depends on comparison, leverage, and visibility. Agency, by contrast, is self-referential. It does not need to be witnessed to be real.

As agency stabilises, people often notice a reduced interest in proving anything. The urge to persuade, convince, or out-argue diminishes. Influence, when it occurs, is quieter and less challenging. It comes from consistency rather than assertion.

This shift can be disorienting, particularly in cultures that equate power with volume or force. Choosing not to engage in power struggles may be misread as weakness or disengagement. In reality, it reflects a different orientation altogether, one that prioritises integrity over impact.

Agency reshapes power by relocating it internally. Authority comes from alignment rather than control. Boundaries are held without escalation. Decisions are made without theatrics. Importantly, this form of power does not require others to change in order to be effective.

This does not mean passivity or withdrawal from the world. It means refusing to participate in dynamics that depend on coercion, performance, or extraction. It allows people to exercise influence where it is invited and to disengage where it is not.

Over time, this orientation creates a different relationship to power altogether, one that is quieter, more sustainable, and far less costly. Power is no longer something to win or defend. It becomes something that is simply exercised, moment by moment, through choice.

Agency as a Stabilising Force

As agency becomes more consistent, it begins to stabilise identity. After prolonged exposure to environments that required adaptation and self-monitoring, many people are left unsure of who they are outside of response. Agency gently restores continuity. Decisions align with values. Actions reflect intention rather than necessity. Over time, a clearer sense of self re-emerges.

This stabilisation is not dramatic. It does not involve reinventing oneself or reclaiming a former version untouched by experience. Instead, it integrates what has been learned with what is no longer required. Endurance gives way to discernment. Compliance gives way to consent. Identity becomes less reactive and more grounded.

Agency also alters how the past is held.

Experiences that once felt disempowering can be understood without defining the present.

The narrative shifts from what happened to me toward how I now choose to live.

The choice to live leads to a life worth living, which reinforces the prior choices that created a sense of agency to begin with.

This does not erase harm, but it reduces its gravitational pull.

The past becomes context rather than constraint.

Importantly, stabilisation does not mean certainty.

There may still be ambiguity, loss, or unresolved questions.

Agency does not eliminate these realities. It provides a steadier platform from which to face them.

It allows people to move forward without requiring closure or validation from the systems that caused harm.

This chapter marks the point at which power is no longer something to recover from others, but something exercised internally.

Agency becomes the organising principle, replacing survival and reaction.

From here, attention can turn outward again, not to endure or adapt, but to speak, create, and choose direction deliberately.

What follows builds on this foundation.

With agency stabilised, voice can return without being defensive.

Boundaries can be articulated without escalation.

A future can be shaped without reference to what once constrained it.

Finding Your Voice

THE STRATEGIST

The Strategist does not speak to be heard.
They speak to shift outcomes.
Silence and speech are both tools.

RIGHT WITH YOU

Speaking Without Defending

For a long time, silence serves a purpose. It protects energy, limits exposure, and reduces risk. In environments shaped by coercion or instability, withholding one's voice can be an act of self-preservation rather than avoidance. Silence is how people survive when speaking carries consequences.

As agency stabilises, the role of silence begins to change. What was once protective can start to feel constraining. The absence of expression becomes noticeable, not because there is pressure to speak, but because the internal sense of alignment has shifted. Silence no longer feels chosen. It feels habitual.

This moment does not arrive with urgency. It arrives as a quiet recognition that one's perspective exists independently of whether it is acknowledged. The need to remain unseen diminishes. The fear attached to being heard softens, even if it does not disappear entirely.

Finding one's voice does not mean speaking immediately or publicly. It begins internally, as permission. Permission to name one's experience accurately, without minimisation or exaggeration. Permission to stop rehearsing explanations for those who are unlikely to listen. Permission to let truth exist without being argued into legitimacy.

What changes at this stage is not volume, but posture. Voice shifts from defensive to declarative. Words are no longer shaped primarily to pre-empt doubt or disbelief. They are shaped by clarity.

This shift can feel vulnerable. Speaking without defending removes familiar armour. It requires trust, not that one will be received perfectly, but that one's experience does not require validation to be real.

This chapter is about that transition. Not from silence to speech, but from guarded expression to owned voice.

Voice Returns Privately First

Before the voice becomes visible, it is reclaimed in private. This stage is easy to overlook, because it leaves little external trace. There are no announcements, no declarations, no audience. Yet it is often here that the most important shift occurs.

Private voice begins as honesty without performance. People stop editing their own thoughts for acceptability. They allow themselves to acknowledge what they know, what they felt, and what they no longer need to explain away. Journals may change tone. Internal narratives soften. Language becomes more precise, less apologetic.

This stage often involves selective expression. People choose carefully who, if anyone, is allowed access to their emerging voice.

Conversations become more intentional. Not everyone needs to hear everything. Trust is rebuilt gradually, based on response rather than expectation.

Reclaiming voice privately also means disentangling truth from outcome.

For a long time, speaking may have been evaluated by what it produced: agreement, resolution, safety. In this phase, expression is valued for its accuracy rather than its effect. Words are allowed to exist without being tasked with fixing anything.

There can be relief in this privacy. It offers space to experiment with language, to find phrasing that feels true without being sharpened for defence. People may notice that they no longer feel compelled to correct misinterpretations immediately or to respond to every distortion. Silence becomes a choice again, not a reflex.

This private reclamation of voice is foundational. It restores authorship before exposure. By the time the voice moves outward, if it does, it does so from a place of internal alignment rather than urgency.

Finding one's voice does not begin with being heard. It begins with listening to oneself, without interruption, negotiation, or doubt.

Speaking Without Anticipating Disbelief

One of the most significant shifts in reclaiming voice occurs when words are no longer shaped around the expectation of disbelief. After prolonged exposure to environments where experiences were questioned, minimised, or reframed, many people learn to pre-empt doubt.

They over-explain. They qualify. They provide context before it is asked for. Their voice becomes defensive before it is even challenged.

As agency stabilises, this pattern begins to loosen. People notice when they are speaking to convince rather than to express.

They become aware of how much energy has been spent anticipating reactions that may never come or that cannot be influenced regardless of preparation.

Speaking without anticipating disbelief does not mean assuming one will be understood. It means releasing responsibility for managing others' responses. Words are offered without being padded, sharpened, or softened to secure acceptance. Truth is allowed to stand without scaffolding.

This shift can feel exposed. Without the familiar armour of explanation, there is a sense of vulnerability; a risk that one's account will be dismissed or misunderstood. But there is also relief. Voice becomes less challenging. Expression feels cleaner, more direct.

Importantly, this does not require confrontation. Speaking without defending is not about insisting on agreement. It is about accuracy. People choose words that reflect their experience, then allow space for response, or not. Silence from others no longer automatically registers as invalidation.

Over time, this approach reshapes self-trust.

When the voice is no longer calibrated to disbelief, it becomes anchored internally.

People stop measuring the legitimacy of their experience by how it is received.

The need to prove fades.

This is where voice begins to feel owned rather than negotiated.

Not because it is louder, but because it is no longer conditional.

Who Gets Access to Your Voice

As voice strengthens, discernment becomes essential. Reclaiming one's voice does not mean offering it indiscriminately. Not every audience is safe, capable, or willing to receive it with integrity. Learning this is not cynicism. It is wisdom earned through experience.

After prolonged exposure to disbelief or distortion, many people feel pressure to finally be heard: to say everything, everywhere, all at once. This impulse is understandable. But unfiltered exposure can recreate harm by placing voice back into environments that misuse, weaponise, or dismiss it.

Discernment asks a different question:

Who has demonstrated the capacity to listen without rearranging my words?

Access is no longer granted by proximity, authority, or expectation. It is granted by response.

Some people listen to reply. Others listen to correct. Some listen only for what confirms their existing narrative. Speaking to these audiences often requires defence, clarification, or emotional labour. All signs that voice is being negotiated rather than expressed.

Protecting your voice does not mean withholding truth. It means choosing context. It means recognising that clarity does not obligate disclosure, and authenticity does not require exposure. Silence, when chosen, can be an expression of agency rather than fear.

This discernment can feel uncomfortable at first, particularly for those conditioned to explain themselves.

Withholding access may trigger guilt or concern about being misunderstood.

But over time, it stabilises. Voice remains intact because it is not constantly tested or defended.

Discernment also restores proportion. Some truths are personal. Some are relational. Some are public.

Not every truth belongs in every space. Choosing where to speak preserves the integrity of what is spoken.

Finding one's voice includes learning where it can land safely and where it does not need to land at all.

When Voice Is No Longer Reactive

When voice is reclaimed from a place of agency, it alters power dynamics without needing to confront them directly. Speech no longer arises from urgency, defence, or the need to correct a narrative in real time. Instead, it is grounded in choice, whether to speak, when to speak, and how much to say.

In reactive environments, the voice is often shaped by pressure. People speak to stop something, to fix something, or to protect themselves from misrepresentation. Words are hurried. The tone is sharpened. Energy is expended anticipating consequences. Even when the content is accurate, the posture remains defensive.

Speaking from an agency changes this posture. There is less need to respond immediately or comprehensively. Silence becomes an option rather than a loss. When words are offered, they are measured and intentional. The absence of urgency reduces escalation.

This shift can be unsettling to those accustomed to extracting reactions. When voice is no longer reactive, it is harder to provoke. Power struggles lose momentum because one side is no longer participating in them. The dynamic changes without announcement.

Importantly, speaking from agency does not mean withholding truth. It means decoupling truth from emotional labour. Words are not used to persuade, appease, or correct others' misunderstandings unless doing so aligns with one's values and capacity.

This form of voice is often quieter, but it carries more weight. It does not rely on repetition or volume. It relies on consistency. Over time, people notice that speech from this place feels steadier, not because it dominates the room, but because it is no longer pulled off-centre by others' reactions.

When the voice is no longer reactive, it becomes difficult to manipulate. It cannot be easily reframed or weaponised because it is not offered into the same transactional space. Power shifts not through confrontation, but through disengagement from the old terms of engagement.

Voice as Authorship, Not Exposure

When voice is reclaimed from a place of agency, it becomes less about being seen and more about authorship. Speaking is no longer an act of exposure. A risk taken in the hope of being believed or validated. It becomes an expression of ownership over one's own story.

Authorship changes the relationship to truth.

The question shifts from:

Will this be accepted?

To:

Is this accurate?

Words are chosen to reflect experience, not to secure agreement. The need to reveal everything dissipates because nothing is being hidden from oneself.

This orientation brings a different kind of freedom. Silence and speech carry equal legitimacy. Choosing not to speak is no longer interpreted as fear or retreat, but as discernment. Choosing to speak is no longer charged with urgency or self-protection, but guided by intention.

Voice, in this form, does not seek to convince. It does not argue for its own reality. It exists without demand. This can feel unfamiliar in cultures that reward disclosure and performance, but it is deeply stabilising. Power remains internal, regardless of response.

Importantly, authorship allows the past to be integrated without being rehearsed. Experiences can be named without being re-lived. Meaning can be made without reopening harm. Voice becomes a way of organising experience, not re-entering it.

This chapter marks the point at which truth is no longer something to defend or explain. It is something to hold. With voice reclaimed in this way, the story belongs fully to the person who lived it, not to those who questioned it, distorted it, or benefited from its silence.

What follows builds on this ownership. Once the voice is no longer defensive, it can be directed outward with purpose, toward contribution, boundary-setting, and the shaping of what comes next.

Reclaiming Direction

THE WITNESS

The Witness holds the truth steady. They stop explaining, justifying, or correcting the record. What is known becomes the compass.

RIGHT WITH YOU

Living Beyond the Harm

There comes a point where the harm no longer sits at the centre of one's life. This does not mean it is forgotten, denied, or minimised. It means it no longer determines the shape of every decision. Attention begins to move forward rather than backward.

This shift can feel unfamiliar. For a long time, energy was directed toward understanding, surviving, recovering, and reclaiming what was lost. Those efforts were necessary. They restored agency and voice. But they were also reactive, shaped by what had already occurred. Reclaiming direction is about something different. It is about choosing how to live now, not in opposition to the past, but independently of it.

The question is no longer:

How do I protect myself from what happened?

But:

What do I want to move toward?

This change is often subtle. People notice that their thinking includes future-oriented curiosity again. Interests resurface. Values feel less abstract. The world begins to widen beyond the boundaries set by harm.

Importantly, moving beyond the harm does not require resolution or closure. Many experiences never receive acknowledgement or repair. Direction does not depend on those outcomes. It depends on internal permission to live fully despite their absence. This chapter explores what it means to let life expand again, to exercise power and voice in service of meaning, contribution, and choice, rather than defence.

When Moving Forward Feels Like Betrayal

One of the quiet tensions that emerges at this stage is the feeling that moving forward somehow betrays what was endured. After investing so much energy in understanding harm, naming patterns, and reclaiming agency, the idea of shifting focus can feel disloyal to one's past self, to the truth of what happened, or to others who are still living within similar conditions.

This feeling is rarely articulated, but it can exert a strong pull. People may worry that stepping into a fuller life diminishes the seriousness of what occurred, or that choosing direction implies forgiveness, acceptance, or indifference. These assumptions can create an internal resistance to growth, even when growth is clearly desired.

What sits beneath this tension is a misunderstanding of meaning. Honouring experience does not require permanent orientation around it. Acknowledging harm does not obligate a lifetime of response.

The significance of what was endured is not measured by how long it governs the present. There can also be fear of losing legitimacy. For a time, identity may have been organised around survival, recovery, or truth-telling. Moving forward can feel like stepping out of a role that provided coherence and validation. Without it, people may wonder who they are allowed to be.

This is not a failure of resolve. It reflects the depth of what was carried. Letting life widen again can feel risky because it introduces the possibility of joy, engagement, and investment, all of which make one vulnerable in new ways. Understanding this tension allows it to loosen. Moving forward is not betrayal. It is the completion of a phase. It signals that the harm no longer requires constant vigilance to be remembered. Direction becomes possible when the past is held with respect, but not with obligation.

When Values Begin to Lead

As direction is reclaimed, something subtle but decisive changes in how decisions are made. Reaction gives way to orientation. Instead of asking what will prevent harm or minimise risk, people begin to ask what aligns with their values, not aspirationally, but practically.

Values at this stage are not abstract ideals. They are felt preferences shaped by experience: a desire for fairness without vigilance, contribution without depletion, connection without compromise. These values are often clarified precisely because harm has made misalignment visible.

When values lead, choices become simpler, even when they are not easy. Decisions are evaluated less by their capacity to avoid discomfort and more by their coherence.

The question shifts from:

Will this protect me?

To:

Does this reflect who I am now?

This shift reduces internal conflict, even when external circumstances remain complex.

Values-led direction also alters tolerance. People become less willing to invest energy in situations that require ongoing self-suppression, explanation, or vigilance. This is not rigidity. It is respect for one's own limits. What once might have been endured out of habit or obligation is now assessed more carefully.

Importantly, values do not demand perfection. They provide orientation, not prescription. People may still make compromises, but those compromises are conscious rather than default. When misalignment occurs, it is noticed earlier and addressed with less self-blame.

Over time, living in accordance with values restores a sense of integrity that prolonged exposure often erodes. Actions feel internally consistent. Direction feels self-authored. Life is no longer organised around what must be avoided, but around what is worth moving toward.

This values-led orientation is what allows power and voice to be exercised sustainably. It anchors forward movement in meaning, rather than reaction and creates the conditions for a life that is shaped by choice rather than constrained by history.

Sustaining Direction Without Returning to Old Patterns

Reclaiming direction is not a one-time achievement. Like agency and voice, it must be sustained, not through constant vigilance, but through ongoing awareness of how old patterns reassert themselves under pressure.

Stress has a way of narrowing focus. In moments of uncertainty or fatigue, familiar survival strategies can resurface: over-functioning, self-silencing, excessive accommodation, or the impulse to manage outcomes that do not belong to you. These returns are not failures. They are reminders of how deeply those patterns were once required.

What changes at this stage is response. Instead of interpreting regression as loss of progress, people recognise it as information. Old patterns are noticed earlier and interrupted more gently. Direction is restored not through self-criticism, but through recalibration.

Sustaining direction also involves respecting limits. Values-led living does not mean constant expansion or productivity. It includes rest, pause, and contraction when needed. Choosing less can be as aligned as choosing more. Direction holds when it allows for fluctuation rather than demanding consistency at all costs.

Another stabilising factor is the capacity to revisit choice.

Direction is not fixed.

Circumstances change, priorities shift, and understanding deepens.

What felt aligned at one stage may require revision later. Sustaining direction means remaining responsive to this evolution without framing it as indecision.

Importantly, direction endures when it is not defined in opposition to the past. When life is organised primarily around not repeating harm, the past retains influence. When direction is shaped by present values and future possibility, the past recedes into context.

This does not mean forgetting what was learned. It means applying that learning without being governed by it. Direction becomes a living practice: flexible, grounded, and resilient, rather than a fixed destination to defend.

Contribution Without Self-Sacrifice

As direction stabilises, many people notice a renewed desire to contribute, not as obligation, redemption, or proof of worth, but as expression. After prolonged periods where energy was consumed by survival and recovery, the impulse to engage meaningfully with the world can feel both welcome and uncertain.

This stage requires care.

In the past, contribution may have been entangled with self-sacrifice.

Giving more, doing more, carrying more were often framed as virtues, even when they came at personal cost.

Reclaiming direction involves disentangling contribution from depletion.

The contribution that emerges from alignment feels different.

It is chosen rather than compelled.

It respects capacity.

It does not require erasure of self in service of others.

People become more selective about where their effort goes and more attentive to whether it is reciprocated, valued, or simply extracted.

This selectivity is not withdrawal. It is discernment.

Contributing from a place of agency means recognising that impact does not require exhaustion, and that care does not require self-abandonment.

Saying no to one form of engagement often makes room for another that is more sustainable.

Direction also reshapes connection.

Relationships formed or renewed at this stage are less likely to be based on shared adversity alone.

They are grounded instead in values, curiosity, and mutual respect.

This shift allows connection to feel generative rather than draining.

Importantly, contribution without self-sacrifice restores dignity.

It affirms that one's time, energy, and voice are finite and valuable.

Engaging with the world becomes a source of meaning rather than obligation, an extension of agency rather than its erosion.

This orientation allows people to step into roles, projects, or communities not because they must, but because they choose to.

Direction, in this sense, is not about narrowing one's world.

It is about participating in it on terms that preserve wholeness.

Direction as Integration

Reclaiming direction is not about replacing one organising principle with another. It is about integration: allowing agency, voice, and values to coexist without competing for dominance. Life is no longer structured around reaction, recovery, or resistance. It is structured around coherence.

At this stage, people often notice a new steadiness. Decisions are made with less internal negotiation. Boundaries are held without explanation. Engagement feels intentional rather than obligatory. The energy once spent managing harm is now available for living. Integration also changes how the past is carried. Experiences of harm are neither erased nor centralised. They inform judgement without dictating direction. Lessons remain, but they no longer require constant reference. The past becomes part of the story, not the author of it. This shift allows people to move through the world with greater ease. They are less reactive to provocation, less compelled to correct misunderstanding, less invested in outcomes that do not align with their values. Direction provides an internal compass that reduces the need for external validation.

Importantly, integration does not imply finality. There may still be moments of uncertainty, grief, or recalibration. But these moments no longer threaten collapse. They are absorbed into a broader sense of self that is resilient without being rigid.

This chapter marks the point where life is no longer organised around what was taken, endured, or survived. It is organised around what is chosen. Direction becomes a lived expression of agency and voice, not something to defend, but something to inhabit.

What follows moves beyond personal restoration and toward legacy. Once direction is reclaimed, attention can turn to how one's experience, insight, and clarity might shape the world beyond the self, without returning to sacrifice or harm.

This Is Not The End

THE AUTHORS

**The Authors no longer live inside the story written for them.
This is not the end.
It is the point of authorship.**

RIGHT WITH YOU

They are not finished because the work continues.

There comes a point where survival is no longer the work.

The body steadies.

The noise recedes.

The questions that once demanded constant answering lose their urgency.

What remains is not resolution, but clarity.

This chapter is written from that place.

Not as a response, not as a defence, and not as a final word, but as authorship.

What happened did not conclude neatly. Systems rarely do. Files close. Processes end. Attention moves on. But the consequences of what unfolded do not obey administrative timelines. They continue in bodies, in careers, in trust recalibrated downward. They continue quietly, long after institutions declare matters resolved.

This is not an indictment. It is an observation.

What becomes visible with distance is not only harm, but design. Patterns that once felt chaotic begin to reveal structure. Decisions that were framed as isolated take shape as coordinated. The burden that was carried privately begins to look collective.

What we resisted at the time: the insistence that nothing was personal, becomes legible only later. Not because the experience lacked impact, but because its impact was never the point. The system offered the appearance of choice while narrowing outcomes: through inaction, sanctioned action, or manufactured inability.

The point was:

- Containment
- Control
- Compliance
- Delay
- Attrition

Survival, then, was not a triumph. It was a condition. A necessary one. Endurance was not chosen because it was noble, but because it was required to remain intact long enough to understand what was happening.

Authorship begins where that necessity ends.

Where Are They Now

What followed did not look like resolution.

For each of the employees from Union A, B & C, life continued in altered form; shaped by what had occurred, constrained by what remained unresolved, and influenced by a shared understanding of how systems behave when challenged.

The employee from **Union A** did not return to institutional employment. Instead, they built outside of it.

The Reckoning Room emerged as both record and response: a platform grounded in lived experience, evidence, and pattern recognition.

What began as documentation became advocacy. The work expanded nationally, then beyond borders, as others recognised their own experiences reflected in its pages.

Some matters resolved. Many did not.

Assistance continues navigating systems designed to exhaust, delay, and discourage. A website is now live, providing a central platform for this work. Alongside it sits ***Silent Saboteurs***, a parallel project that documents the events in memoir form. The work continues because the conditions that necessitated it are still present.

The employee from **Union B** redirected their focus toward rebuilding professional footing interrupted by years of workplace turmoil and prolonged post-employment harassment. A long-deferred law degree is nearing completion.

Alongside this, they prepared the launch of ***Pink Collar Workers***: a platform shaped by both legal training and lived harm.

They also commenced a counselling qualification, not as a gesture toward healing narratives, but as a practical response to what they had seen repeatedly fail inside formal systems.

The employee from **Union C** withdrew from institutional spaces altogether. What sustained them initially was not process or recognition, but creative practice. Photography became a means of stabilisation: a way to re-establish presence after profound disorientation. Their workers' compensation matter remains unresolved. Like many others, it continues in parallel with life, rather than concluding it.

Taken together, these trajectories do not form a success story. They form a pattern.

Distance from institutions made reflection possible. Time clarified what had been obscured. What emerged was not closure, but insight: harm was not incidental, nor isolated, nor accidental. It followed recognisable rules. It repeated across roles, organisations, and jurisdictions.

Collective Voice

What became clear over time was that authorship was never singular.

Each of these trajectories emerged independently, shaped by different constraints and decisions.

Yet they converged around the same realisation: what we experienced was not aberration, nor personality conflict, nor misfortune. It was structural. And once seen as such, it could no longer be unseen.

Authorship, in this sense, is not about ownership of narrative. It is about responsibility for meaning.

The act of writing, whether through formal publication, advocacy, legal study, creative practice, or quiet withdrawal, was not undertaken to persuade institutions to change. It was undertaken to prevent the rewriting of what had already occurred.

To hold memory where systems relied on attrition. To maintain coherence where fragmentation was incentivised.

This is where the plural matters.

Because what sustains systems of harm is not only power, but isolation. Each individual is encouraged to believe their experience is abnormal, their reaction excessive, their expectations unreasonable. The remedy offered is often personal resilience, reframing, or silence, rarely structural accountability.

What disrupted that pattern was not confrontation, but comparison.

Across different unions, roles, jurisdictions, and outcomes, the same mechanics appeared. The same reliance on delay. The same narrowing of language. The same emphasis on procedure over substance. The same quiet repositioning of responsibility downward, away from decision-makers and onto individuals expected to absorb the cost.

Seen alone, each story could be dismissed. Seen together, dismissal failed.

Authorship, then, became an act of accumulation.

Not to collapse differences, but to preserve them within a shared frame. Not to demand belief, but to make disbelief untenable. Not to seek vindication, but to ensure that what was learned did not remain privately held.

This is the point at which experience stops being testimonial and becomes diagnostic.

And it is also the point at which authorship stops being personal and becomes transferable.

Because once patterns are visible, they can be taught.

Once language is decoded, it can be shared.

Once the mechanics of containment are understood, people can recognise them earlier, and make different choices about engagement, exit, or resistance.

This does not guarantee better outcomes. But it does reduce disorientation.

It gives people a way to orient themselves without internalising blame. It offers a vocabulary for experiences that are otherwise flattened into grievance or pathology. And it creates continuity between those who came before and those who will encounter similar systems in the future.

This is not solidarity as a slogan.

It is literacy as inheritance.

What Changed and What Did Not

What changed was proximity.

Distance allowed breath. Distance allowed language to return. Distance made thinking possible again. It revealed how much energy had been consumed not by the work itself, but by managing instability, anticipation, and fear.

What did not change were the structures that produced the harm. The same mechanisms remained available. The same incentives persisted. The same vocabulary continued to sanitise outcomes that were anything but neutral.

Understanding this was not liberating in the way self-help narratives promise. It did not dissolve grief or retroactively restore what was lost. But it did remove confusion. And that mattered.

Clarity does not heal everything. But it stabilises. It prevents self-erasure. It stops people from contorting themselves to fit explanations that were never true.

From Experience to Examination

This is the point where the work changes form.

What has been recorded here is experience: lived, documented, corroborated across different contexts.

What follows is not a continuation of memoir. It is analysis. Because once a pattern can be named, it can be studied.

The next phase of this work is not about telling what happened again.

It is about understanding how it happened, why it repeated, and how ordinary people were positioned inside systems that claimed neutrality while practising containment.

It is about rules that are unwritten, timelines that are weaponised, processes that exhaust rather than resolve, and language that obscures responsibility while appearing procedural.

It is about recognising that if you are pushed onto someone else's timeline, you are not simply delayed, you are being displaced from your own future.

This Is Not the End

This chapter does not close the story.

It hands it forward.

What follows is an examination of the games that were being played, the boards on which they occurred, and the rules that governed outcomes long before any individual move was made.

This is not about blame.

It is about literacy.

Not everyone needs to play these games.

But no one should be harmed by them without understanding how they work.

This is not the end.

It is the point at which the story can finally be examined.

Tip:

If you permit someone to push you onto their timeline, you are losing opportunities for your future and potential new timelines you haven't yet imagined.

www.ingramcontent.com/pod-product-compliance
Lightning Source LLC
LaVergne TN
LVHW012340100826
845148LV00018B/2869

* 9 7 8 1 7 6 4 6 2 7 2 1 4 *